GLORY
TO
GLORY

A Devotional Journey Through Scripture

Contents

Thank you to all who have provided support and wisdom in producing this publication.

A special thanks are also due to Karen and Sam for their extensive feedback and attention to detail that have greatly shaped what now lies before you.

Introduction

Over the course of human history, one would be hard pressed to find a more influential book than the Bible. Much of Western civilisation has been built upon its contents, including our system of proportionate justice, our focus on caring for the vulnerable in society and a morality which values human life. The Bible's impact is personal too, with countless lives having been changed through what it reveals about the person of Jesus and his message of forgiveness, love and hope.

It's because of this personal impact that certain governments have banned its existence, lest their citizens trust and submit to an authority other than them. Ownership of the Bible has carried (and in some places continue to carry) the very real possibility of death, yet for many it's a risk they're willing to take. Others, knowing the significance of what the Bible teaches, remain willing to risk their lives in order that the whole world can read its message.

The Bible is rightly intended to be a central part of each believer's spiritual life. However, its scale and the unusual literary styles found within, can make it quite daunting. For example, should we start from the beginning and read it through to the end like a novel? Are we supposed to keep the laws given to Israel? If Jesus has come and changed everything, then why even bother to read the Old Testament? Despite being surrounded by various different translations, and websites which enable us to study the Bible for free, biblical literacy continues to decline, even amongst Christians. Many are aware of the great stories in the Bible (David and Goliath, Daniel in the lion's den, the cross and resurrection, etc) but often they lack an understanding of how those stories fit within the larger biblical narrative.

These comments aren't designed to condemn, but rather highlight issues we face as Christians that we should seek to address. The fifteen-hundred or so pages which comprise the Bible are God's revelation to humanity about who he is, our place within a relationship with him and how he's worked (and continues to work) within creation. It's the foundational text that our faith is built upon, informing our theology and our view of the world, a view which is often the opposite of what our culture teaches. The historical events recorded, particularly the events of the gospels, are evidence for the existence of God, assuring us that our hope is in something substantial, and not just based upon a wish that there be something beyond this life.

For these reasons and more, the Bible is a book we should desire to know more deeply and so they have formed the basis for three aims which I intend this resource to fulfil.

To succinctly walk the reader through the main narrative of the Bible

Most reading plans that go through the Bible take place over a year, and although these are immensely valuable, they require a commitment that not everyone's prepared to make - particularly those who find reading less than enjoyable. In this resource, the narrative has been condensed to forty sets of readings roughly ten minutes in length, selected with the aim of focusing attention on the key points of the narrative.

To highlight the key themes of scripture and their interconnectedness

One of the most remarkable aspects of the Bible is that despite being made up of over 60 books and having been written over hundreds of years by various authors, the text fits together so neatly. Themes of sin, redemption, atonement, grace and many others are found throughout the Bible, but jumping in and out means that it's easy to lose sight of either their consistency (the grace of God and the call to put our trust in him alone) or how they progress over time (God's presence and how we approach him in worship). By moving through the story of scripture in such a concise way, it is intended that you will be better able to notice the prevalence of key themes such as these.

To provide knowledge that illuminates the Bible in new ways

The Bible is written for us, but not to us. This means that there are many cultural and historical aspects that we can overlook. For example, when we read of the Israelites worshiping idols instead of God, we tend to impose our own monotheistic worldview onto their actions and assume that the Israelites are rejecting the existence of God. This interpretation is likely to be mistaken (p14). Another example would be failing to understand the significance of temples in the ancient world and how they differ from modern churches (p18).

Throughout the book are various tangential explanations which aim to illuminate these sorts of issues as well as briefly introduce some key theological and apologetic discussions. Collectively, they will provide you with key foundational knowledge that should bring greater clarity to the passages you encounter.

<u>Layout</u>

The majority of this book is divided into forty sections each comprising a list of readings, a short reflection and an additional explanatory section or two. The first set of readings are chosen so that over the duration of the book, one would journey through the main elements of the biblical narrative. Although they vary in length, the majority should take between five and ten minutes to read through. Generally, these readings also form the basis for the subsequent reflection. In brackets are additional readings for those who wish to explore the context of the main passages in more detail.

The content is laid out in a modular way so that people can engage with the material in the way they wish. For some people, that will involve going through the main set of readings and the reflection over a 15-minute period. Others will want to engage with every single page and scripture reference. As the reader it is for you to choose an approach that works for you.

Although present in some, most reflections don't end with instructions for what you as the reader should do in response. God speaks uniquely to each of us and therefore, rather than prescribing how you should react, I would rather leave that decision to you. If you're unsure how to respond to a given reflection, then a simple suggestion would be to highlight any key points that jump out to you about God or yourself and spend some time reflecting upon them.

However you choose to make use of what has been written, my prayer is that God will meet with you and reveal himself to you in new and exciting ways.

<u>Notes</u>

At this point, I believe it's worth pausing to highlight a couple of points. Firstly, a distinction needs to be made between the god of the Bible (Yahweh) and the false gods who were also worshipped. For clarity, all references to the former use a capitalized G, whilst those beginning with a lower-case g refer to either false gods or the general concept of gods.

The Bible also contains several characters whose names are changed by God due to a change in relationship with him. Throughout this book, the more familiar name is typically used when referencing these people. Below are the people concerned with the chosen name given in bold:

Abram / **Abraham**

Sarai / **Sarah**

Jacob / Israel

Simon / **Peter**

Saul / **Paul** (this renaming wasn't performed by God – Acts 13:9)

Finally, the dating of events that the Bible records is an evolving area of study as new archaeological information is uncovered and, of course, weighed with what the Bible describes. Although it's hard to ever claim that any chosen date is certain beyond doubt or universally accepted by historians, most of the events following the rule of David are typically able to be dated within a very narrow range of error.

However, as we move further into the past, it becomes significantly more challenging to find consensus. The Exodus is typically dated to either the mid-fifteenth or thirteenth century BC, a decision which then affects the length of time that Israel was led by Judges. Beyond this too is the question of how long the Israelites were in slavery in Egypt and how long a period the events of Genesis 1-11 took place within.

It's beyond the scope of this resource to analyse these arguments, but the fact that no consensus yet exists demonstrates that there's evidence (both inside and outside the Bible) for a range of positions. For these reasons, I have refrained from making specific claims about dates for events that took place before the temple of Solomon was built. The most important point to understand is that the events recorded in the Bible have taken place. However, if you're interested in this field, then I encourage you to explore the different positions held and the evidence supporting them in order to draw your own conclusions.

Understanding the Bible

The Bible can be a complex and confusing book to read, and therefore people often struggle to identify the points that the original author was making. Additionally, people can also find it hard to retain what they have read and discovered. Something that can help with both problems is the use of short questions such as those detailed below. Not only can they help us to focus on the main lessons of the passage, but when we identify something for ourselves it becomes far easier to retain that knowledge than if we were simply told it. Accompanying each question is a short description and example thoughts from reading Mark 5:1-20.

What is the passage describing?

Having read a passage through, it's helpful to pause and reflect on what is being described, perhaps coming up with a short summary. Similarly, breaking the text down into a series of steps can help to make the smaller details in the passage stand out more clearly.

Mark 5:1-20 records an instance where Jesus travelled to the Decapolis (a Gentile region) and healed a demon possessed man (demoniac) who had been ostracised from the community. The demons recognise who Jesus is and so beg to enter the nearby pig herd who rush into the lake and die. The people hear what has happened and beg Jesus to leave. The man begs to go with Jesus, but Jesus commands him to stay and tell others what God has done for him.

What does this Passage Teach Me?

Every passage of the Bible has been included to teach us something that the author felt was important for us to know. However, because of the broad nature of this question, it may be helpful to focus on the three areas of revelation outlined below:

God: The Bible is the primary means by which God reveals himself to us. Therefore, we should always be looking for aspects of God's character that the author wanted to highlight.

Throughout the passage Jesus is revealed to be compassionate towards those who suffer, have authority over the forces of evil and desire that people hear about him. Because the demons acknowledge him as Son of the Most High God, what is revealed regarding Jesus can be understood as describing God.

Humanity: As well as teaching us about God, the Bible provides us with insights about the nature of humanity. Some of these, though important, can be difficult to hear such as our sinfulness and tendency to replace God in our lives with various idols. However, the Bible also reveals to us wonderful truths about how we've been formed in God's image, the immense value we each have and our position as God's adopted children.

Despite the man being kept away from the rest of the villagers, Jesus demonstrates his value before God and shows that he's still able to approach and be met by God. There is also the question of why the villagers are so desperate to get rid of Jesus after these events? Perhaps they're terrified by what they have seen (the power and work of God can certainly be scary to non-believers), but maybe they're just angry that their pigs are now dead. Following Jesus isn't without cost but it's a cost many are unprepared to make.

What God desires of us: Finally, we should consider anything that the passage is revealing about what God desires of us. At the heart of these considerations are the two great commandments, that we love God and one another. Throughout the Bible, different ways in which we should live out these commands are highlighted such as obediently following God and demonstrating justice, fairness, forgiveness and love to those we meet. Conversely, there are many passages which discourage or prohibit certain behaviours that would harm our relationships with God and our neighbours.

Having been healed Jesus's command to the man is to go about telling others what God has done for him. This is something that all of his followers should be excited to do, joyfully sharing the good news of the gospel.

Although it's possible to answer these questions when studying small sections in isolation, it's important to recognise that the Bible is divided into individual books which are often focused on several key themes. By reading a book the whole way through, these points of emphasis can become more noticeable and thus easier to identify. For example, if you were to read through a chapter of Joshua you might be struck by the miracles recorded or impressed by the power of God. What would be harder to spot though, from just one passage, are key themes such as God's faithfulness to his promises and the continual call for the people to remain obedient to his commands.

How does this fit with the rest of the Bible?

There are two main benefits to asking this question. Firstly, by looking for connections between different passages, we may gain a better understanding of what the author was conveying to their audience. This is particularly the case when we identify Old Testament imagery and quotations used by New Testament authors.

Another reason is to guard against making false conclusions. Although certain aspects of God's character are revealed progressively, overall, the Bible is consistent regarding who God is and what he expects of us. Therefore, when we find passages which seem to contradict one another or teach something that conflicts with what we already know about God, it's helpful to spend more time studying them, humbly allowing God to correct any interpretations or assumptions that are incorrect

The demoniac is presented as someone who is ritually unclean according to Old Testament laws. Such people were unable to approach God in worship but here, and elsewhere during his ministry, Jesus meets those people. Once we identify Jesus as God, the gospel narratives can be viewed as demonstrating that these purity regulations, which have been necessary for approaching God up to this point, are being removed. As Christians we no longer need to keep these portions of the law as they have been fulfilled through the work of Jesus.

What will change now that I've read this passage?

The Bible is given not just to educate us, but to transform us. Therefore, we should always consider how our lives will be impacted by what we've read. We often limit this to thinking about how our actions will change, but the transformation God desires is far deeper, involving a complete renewal of our minds (Rom 12:2). The Bible should affect our motivations, priorities and desires, forming the basis through which we view the world and its problems.

We're called to imitate the love of Jesus, and therefore we should seek to treat those marginalised by society in the same way as he did the demon possessed man. That may involve recognising our own shortcomings in this area or identifying ways in which we can demonstrate this love more clearly. In terms of God altering our perspectives, we can be reassured that God loves us too, irrespective of how we see ourselves or how we're treated by others. A final point is understanding that we don't need to be sent somewhere 'special' by God to serve him but can minister to people wherever we find ourselves. In the case of the demoniac that was exactly what God desired of him.

Questions of Indeterminable Depth

Whenever I look through the Bible with others, I'm struck by what they notice that I either overlook, or don't have the ability to identify, because of a lack of knowledge (such as an inability to read ancient Greek). The responses looking at this passage from Mark are my own thoughts and whilst reading it yourself you may have been struck by completely different things. For me, this is what makes reading the Bible so exciting! The idea that there's always something more to discover.

At the back of this book is a section that highlights some simple tips for interpreting each of the different literary styles found within the Bible. Hopefully, through them, your times reading the Bible will be more fruitful as you begin to see and discover new truths that until this point have been hidden.

Our Questions

When we spend time reading the Bible, we're each guaranteed to come across passages that we struggle to understand. In these moments people can sometimes feel a sense of shame or inadequacy, as if they should know everything already. However, Jesus was always willing to answer the many questions that his followers had, even those he'd already addressed or that to us may appear obvious. We should seek to imitate both the disciples, excitedly pursuing deeper levels of understanding, and Jesus, patiently supporting and bringing teaching as we engage with one another.

If we're reading in a group, then it may be that someone else can address our questions. However, if alone, then we will need to look further afield. Fortunately, just as the body of Christ includes those gifted in worship, prophecy and leadership, there are also individuals who have been blessed with a deep knowledge of the scriptures. Various resources and commentaries have been written by such people which can both clarify and illuminate the Bible in new ways.

Key Concepts of Scripture

Over the following pages are brief introductions to six concepts that are found throughout scripture. Frequent references are made to different parts of the Bible and therefore, it may be helpful to refer back to this section as you encounter the events described, particularly if they are unfamiliar to you.

Covenant

A covenant was an agreement from the ancient world similar to a modern-day contract. They could be made between anyone, however most covenants in the Bible are either Royal-Grant or Suzerain-Vassal covenants. Both involved people of different social standings, usually a king (which in the Bible is God) and his subject (vassal).

A Royal-Grant had no conditions attached to it. For example, a king may decide to give a piece of land to one of his subjects as a reward for their service or, as is the case with Abraham, as an act of grace (an undeserved blessing). Something assumed with this form of covenant is that the subject will remain under the protection of the king. Therefore, if someone sought to harm them, the king wo expected to defend them.

Alternatively, a Suzerain-Vassal covenant required the vassal to abide by a series of rules. Adherence led to rewards whilst disobedience resulted in punishment. These conditions and outcomes were stipulated within the covenant document. An example of this type of arrangement is the Sinaitic Covenant given to Moses and the nation of Israel.

Messiah

Messiah is a term found in the Old Testament that refers to a king or High Priest. The Messiah (Christ in the New Testament) is an extension of this basic definition that means the anointed one. It is used to identify an individual from the line of David who would be king of Israel and usher in a Messianic age. Christians believe that Jesus was the Messiah.

Most prophecies concerning the Messiah were given in the centuries surrounding the Babylonian exile. Throughout this period, the people longed for the same sort of national prosperity seen during David's reign and, therefore, the idea of Messiah became synonymous with a hope for national restoration. However, God's purpose for the Messiah wasn't worldly prosperity, but spiritual reconciliation: the conquest of sin and death. Once we recognise this, it becomes clear that the Messiah's roles could only have been carried out by God himself. The arm of Yahweh and the suffering servant of Isaiah are seen not as humans, but God himself coming down to rescue his people from the bondage of sin.

Polytheism and Mesopotamian Religion[1]

Western religious beliefs are comprised mostly of monotheistic faith (the worship of one god) or no faith at all. Therefore, very few of us will understand the polytheistic (many gods) worldview held by people in the ancient world. Although the most basic difference between monotheism and polytheism is the number of gods they acknowledge, the consequences of this difference are far-reaching.

Gods were arranged into a hierarchy, often under the headship of one supreme god, but each possessing their own spheres of influence. Worshippers would approach gods based on these spheres. For example, praying to a god who wielded power over weather when concerned over the wellbeing of their crops. However, these spheres often overlapped considerably, and therefore there was typically more than one god who could be approached for a given request.

Citizens of the ancient world didn't hold to three, four or even a million gods. There was no way of knowing precisely how many gods existed, and therefore to deny a god's existence was a huge leap of faith. When Jonah arrived at Nineveh and declared that some god they had never heard of was about to destroy them, they didn't laugh him out of town, but instead sought to appease this god's wrath by repenting of the sins they were told they had committed. Similarly, when the Assyrian army were camped outside Jerusalem, the general didn't deny the existence of Israel's God, or any of the gods worshipped by the peoples they had conquered. Rather, he denied their power compared to his own gods. Another consequence of this attitude was syncretism – the process by which foreign deities were incorporated into an existing culture. It's for this reason that certain gods were worshipped in several locations. Not only was denial of a god's existence not an option, but a new deity meant a new opportunity to benefit from the power of the gods.

[1] For more information on this topic, and the discussion on temples below, I encourage you to engage with the writings of John H Walton, specifically: Ancient Near Eastern Thought and the Old Testament

The gods were more powerful than humans but possessed many of the same emotions and flaws as their worshippers. Gods were inconsistent and irrational, prone to fits of rage, jealousy, etc. They weren't moral examples to follow and were dependent on humans to meet their needs. Failing to do so could lead to divine retribution. However, provided those needs were met, worship of other gods was permissible.

Another key distinction arises from how the ancients viewed what took place in the world. In their eyes, there was no separation of physical and spiritual. Instead, everything was connected to the spiritual realm and therefore had a divine cause, even if the cause couldn't be determined. This was also a commonly held belief in Israel. However, being a monotheistic culture, they could attribute everything to one god. All justice and injustice flowed from God, all blessings and suffering likewise. Their views of God's influence aren't fully affirmed by the rest of scripture, but it helps us to better understand the writings of the psalmist and other wisdom literature which connect God to everything.

One of the most confusing things about the Old Testament narrative is that the Israelites continually appear to stop believing in God and turn instead to worshipping the gods of the surrounding pagan nations. When we encounter these passages, it's easy to impose our own worldview onto a group who lived three thousand years prior. Western society is largely monotheistic with people believing in either one god, or not believing in any gods at all. Therefore, when we see the Israelites worshiping Baal, we tend to assume that they have stopped believing in the existence of their own God. However, the polytheistic culture of the day makes this an unlikely reading. What is far more likely to be happening is that the people are looking to other gods to help them, *because they believe those gods are more capable.* They still believe God exists, but they don't trust his faithfulness, lovingkindness or power in the way God intends. They certainly don't believe his claim to be the only god. Instead they turn to Baal or Asherah or Molech. They are a spiritually adulterous people (Jeremiah 3:1-9, Ezekiel 16).

These attitudes are no less serious than modern unbelief. The first commandment God gave to Israel was to worship no one other than him, and the covenant promises were dependent on them accepting this monotheistic worldview. However, the command to do this was clearly incredibly challenging and the Old Testament repeatedly demonstrates that, influenced by their leaders and the surrounding nations, the Israelites largely failed to fully embrace this change.

Sacrifice[1]

The Bible is full of the language of sacrifice. It's how the Israelites in the Old Testament atoned for their sins and remained in relationship with God, and it's how the New Testament authors made sense of what Jesus accomplished upon the cross. Sacrifice is often misunderstood though. Many consider sacrifice to be solely about killing an animal and therefore can overlook additional elements of the offering process.

Several stages of an Old Testament offering are identifiable. First the worshipper brought an animal before the Lord. They laid their hand upon the animal (Lev 1:4) in the same way as the people did when they ordained the Levites (a tribe of Israel) as priests (Num 8:10). Therefore, just as the priests were appointed to represent the people before God, the animal was appointed to represent the worshipper before God.

Next the animal was killed, and its blood collected. However, death alone didn't make atonement for sins. Instead, the priest was required to distribute the blood on various altars according to the offering being given. The animal was not specifically being punished for the sins of the people, but death was necessary to obtain its blood and, in particular, perform the next stage of the offering.

Having been killed, the animal was appropriately cut with specific portions burnt on the altar in the fire of God (Lev 9:24). The animal transformed into smoke, rose to the heavens and was therefore brought into the presence of God. Through the 'priestly work' of the animal, the worshipper was able to approach God in a way that wasn't possible without death. However, instead of their own death, the worshipper approached through the death of an animal.

The final stage of the offering involved eating any of the animal portions that weren't burnt. At the end of most offerings, it was the priests who ate this meal. However, after the establishment of the Sinaitic Covenant, worshippers were able to make a peace offering which enabled them to enjoy this meal within the tabernacle, the house of God. The death, resurrection and ascension of Jesus fulfilled for all time what the temple rituals could only do temporarily. This is something that will be looked at in more detail at a later point.

[1] For more information on this topic I would point you towards the works of James Jordan and Peter Leithart as well as the Leviticus series from the Theopolis podcast in which these concepts were covered extensively.

<u>Sin</u>

Sin is a term that for most people is synonymous with evil, morally wrong acts, meaning that even people with no religious affiliation, would generally feel offended if they were told their lifestyle was sinful. Sin does, of course, cover actions that are morally wrong, but if that's all that sin means then we run into difficulty when condemning actions that have no discernible negative effects. What is sinful about gambling? Is it even sinful? Is there a difference between playing roulette and buying a raffle ticket at a school fair? In Romans 14:23, Paul declares that everything not done in faith is sin. Well what does this mean then? How can something be sinful for one person and not for another?

It's beyond the ambition of this short section to head too far down this rabbit hole, but hopefully it's becoming clear that the definition of sin must be more complex than just 'bad things'. In the Greek, the word for sin conveys a falling short or missing of the mark. This certainly includes the moral element of rejecting God's commands, but it can also describe a failure to live in line with our God given vocation. Some vocations are for all people such as the worship of God (Rom 1:18-25) and the responsibilities that come with bearing his image. However, others are for specific groups. For example, we aren't required to observe the Sabbath in the same way as the Israelites were expected to, but we are called to use our God given gifts to spread his kingdom. A failure to do this is sin.

Many actions deemed sinful also stem from deeper problems of idolatry where we reject the rule of God and instead begin to worship and serve other things. For example, we have an affair (sin), because of our desire for sexual satisfaction (idol). In our modern culture, most sins described in the Bible that people argue about are those that conflict with our cultural desire for personal satisfaction through sexual gratification, love and power. Each of these has a place within God's creation, yet idolatry elevates them from their rightful place under the authority of God to a position above him and from this elevated position sinful actions tend to flow. For example, exploitation, deceit and envy are just some sins which may flow from idolising power.

When discussing whether actions are sinful, we can sometimes be overly concerned with demonstrating that an action is inherently good or bad through examining specific proof-texts. However, approaching sin in this way ignores the fact that what's more important than the negative consequences of sin is the person (God) who we are sinning against. Ultimately, every sin, even those which seem not to affect anyone else are still a rejection of God. Another danger though, is that we overlook principles of conduct found throughout scripture and the underlying idolatry behind desires. The Bible never talks about raffle tickets, or roulette wheels, but talks a lot about making good use of what God has given us, and not loving money. To conclude that playing roulette is always fine because they aren't explicitly mentioned is to ignore this more important principle about our attitudes to wealth. Moving back to our statement from Paul, what he's trying to get across to his readers is that they need to consider the motivations for their actions. As Christians they are called to worship God alone and therefore if, when presented with a choice, they decide to do something without being confident their actions are in line with God's intentions, then they are making themselves a god. Prioritising their own desires over God's. Paul isn't speaking about whether the action itself is sinful, *and therefore he certainly isn't saying that anything is ok provided we think it's ok*, he's instead declaring the individual's attitude as sinful.

Temple[1]

People often think temples are just the ancient equivalent of churches. However, to ancient worshippers they were far more significant. Firstly, a temple wasn't just a meeting place but was their god's dwelling place on earth: a place where heaven and earth intersected. This idea is clearly demonstrated in the temples of Israel which served as both the dwelling place of God and offered a way for the sacrifices of the people to ascend to God. In this way the tabernacle too was a temple.

From this definition, it also follows that a temple doesn't have to be a building. This explains why John described Jesus, God in human form, as a temple (John 2:21). Likewise, being indwelt by the Holy Spirit, we too are thought of as temples (1 Cor 6:19). God dwelling within us would have been unimaginable to a person from the ancient world but is a key reason why our means of worship is able to be so drastically different from the ways required of Israel. Another point to consider is the role of a temple in a god's work. Temples were the centre of rule for a deity, from which they influenced the world around them. Therefore, as temples of the Holy Spirit, we too can consider ourselves as the points from which God's kingdom spreads across the earth. Whenever we go out into the world, we carry a part of heaven with us; bringing the love, power and forgiveness of God to those we meet.

[1] See note on p14

1. Creation

Genesis 1:1 – Genesis 2:3, Psalm 139

For all who are being led by the Spirit of God, these are sons of God. For you have not received a spirit of slavery leading to fear again, but you have received a spirit of adoption as sons by which we cry out, "Abba! Father!" The Spirit Himself testifies with our spirit that we are children of God, and if children, heirs also, heirs of God and fellow heirs with Christ, if indeed we suffer with Him so that we may also be glorified with Him. (Romans 8:14-17) [1]

Who am I? Do I matter? Am I loved?

Three big questions. Three questions we can each wrestle with, our answers shaped through what we are taught and experience, including how others respond to us. Our conclusions to these questions can come to define our lives and therefore it should come as no surprise that the Bible, God's revelation to us about who he is and who we are, provides us with its own answers from the very beginning.

We are each made in the image of God (Gen 1:27), set apart from the rest of creation to both serve and be in relationship with him. Through relationship we are welcomed into his family as adopted sons and daughters of God (John 1:12), heirs to an imperishable inheritance (1 Peter 1:4) and assured of our future resurrection (John 11:25).

We are each here for a reason, known by God before birth. His thoughts towards us are more numerous than grains of sand. We are God's masterpiece (Eph 2:10). He has a specific plan for our lives and provides us with all we need to accomplish this plan (Heb 13:20-21).

We are each loved with an unfailing love (Psalm 100:5). A love that pre-dates the world (Eph 1:4) and led Jesus to give his own life for us (John 3:16, Rom 5:8). A love that isn't dependant on what we can offer him or how good a life we lead, but a love that instead flows from a God who is the definition of love (1 John 4:8).

The questions we began with can be life defining, so let your life be defined by the answers God speaks.

[1] All scripture quotations are taken from the NASB.

The Account of Creation

Throughout the Bible there are few passages that have been debated more than the opening chapter of Genesis. Many interpretations exist, however below are overviews of several popular viewpoints. These are deliberately short, generic summaries and therefore there will also be people who hold positions located between those described.

Young Earth Creationism

Young Earth Creationism interprets the text as we would understand a historical statement made today and therefore teaches that the earth was created within six twenty-four-hour days, around six thousand years ago. Modern scientific theories of creation are either incorrect or based on God creating the world with the appearance of age (for example it would have been odd to create every tree as a sapling).

Old Earth Creationism

In this view the creation account is seen as more symbolic. The days refer to undefined periods of time with the text less concerned with describing how God created the universe than it is with exploring who was behind creation, why there is a creation and our role as humans within creation. Science can explain how God has ordained the world to function and the processes which he used to bring it into existence. A related view considers verse one to be describing a creation billions of years ago, with the remainder of the chapter detailing some form of transformative 'creation' of a pre-existing planet.

Functional Creation

A recent viewpoint which interprets the creation account as establishing the functionality of the universe, based on textual evidence that the ancients viewed creation in those terms. To claim that a god didn't create the universe would have been ridiculous to people living in the ancient world. They were instead more concerned with knowing that the world was ordered in a way that meant it wasn't going to just stop working. The first chapters of Genesis emphasise the identity and character of the person responsible for creation whilst also addressing the ancient reader's concerns. They are taught that the sun will continue to rise, a cow will always give birth to a cow, and the water above won't suddenly fall down upon them.

Further Reading

Due to their concise nature, each of these summaries may have given rise to a range of additional questions. If this is the case, then you may find it helpful to spend time exploring these views further through some of the many works which have been written on the first two perspectives or the writings of John H Walton on the latter.

A Literal Understanding

Something that has been intentionally left out of each description, is the idea of literal interpretation. Each of the views above can claim to be a literal interpretation because a literal understanding doesn't depend on what the passage means to me, but on what it meant to the original audience. Culture, textual context and literary style are all factors which influence how a text should be understood. If I told you that it was "raining cats and dogs last night", what is the literal understanding of that statement? Perhaps a miracle occurred, or a plane dropped a crate of pets, but what's more likely is that I'm using a well-established phrase to describe a significant amount of rainfall. The challenge we have when interpreting the Bible is determining what the text would have meant to an ancient audience.

Science vs Faith

In recent years notable atheists such as Richard Dawkins have regularly advocated the position that science and religion are in some way incompatible. Although certain views of scripture will lead to conflict, it's certainly not the case that the two are diametrically opposed. Plenty of scientists are faithful Christians and view what they see in science as testimony of the existence of God (Romans 1:20).

Science is concerned with the measurement of observable phenomena and therefore cannot make claims about whether a spiritual entity such as God does or doesn't exist. In a similar way, although the Bible can teach us much about things such as morality, the value of human life and beauty in ways that science cannot, it wasn't written to be a science textbook describing the laws of quantum physics or the methods by which DNA is replicated. Science presents us with processes which govern the world. The Bible reveals that behind each of these is a God who established the universe, whether over six days, or six billion days.

The Image of God

God created man in His own image, in the image of God He created him; male and female He created them. (Gen 1:27).

All humans are made in the image of God. This detail has far reaching ramifications for our theology, philosophy and system of ethics, some of which are only just coming to light as we understand more about what a god's image conveyed to an ancient readership. Below are several simple principles that we should each recognise.

Our Role as Image-Bearers

As humans we're distinct from the rest of creation. In the ancient world an image of a king acted to represent his authority over his kingdom when absent, whilst an image of a god within a temple served as a means through which worshippers could interact with their god. Therefore, as image-bearers, we can view ourselves as having been commissioned to serve God in both an earthly sense through ruling and subduing creation (Gen 1:28) and a spiritual one as we reflect God to those around us.

Not a Physical Representation of God

The image of God isn't describing a physical likeness, but a spiritual one. We're capable of being in a relationship with God, something unique within creation, and possess a spirit that transcends our physical bodies. This image also means that we have an innate understanding of morality (Rom 2:14-15) and a longing for blessings (love, acceptance, self-worth) which can only be fulfilled through relationship with God.

We are *Each* Made in God's Image

This idea was one of the key beliefs which underpinned the abolitionist movement, who recognized there was no biblical justification for a slave trade that treated other humans as inferior. Our attitudes towards others should be similarly grounded in this truth. That rather than defining people by ethnicity, sex, class or any other categories, we primarily see every person on our planet as having been uniquely and lovingly created by a God who died in order to have a relationship with them. This view is at the heart of traditional Christian teaching on subjects such as abortion and euthanasia, as is the understanding that we should strive to treat everyone with the love Jesus thinks them worthy of.

2. Sin Enters the World

Genesis 2:8 – 3:24, Psalm 51

(2 Samuel 11:1 – 12:9) – Additional reading as described on page 7

One morning as a child, at breakfast on New Year's Day, my parents asked, "What are you giving up this year?". "Sin" I replied. Making sure I was being extra polite to those around the table, everything was going wonderfully until my brother sitting opposite accidentally kicked me. Naturally, I responded by kicking him back much firmer and with far more anger. I think I'd kept my resolution for about ten minutes!

Sin is something that we struggle with every day: within our homes and outside, surrounded by others or by ourselves. In the Bible, David was the king of Israel who most faithfully obeyed God, yet even he is shown to be someone who fell far short of perfection. In probably his worst act as king he abused his authority in order to sleep with a married woman and, having gotten her pregnant, concealed his crime by having her husband killed. The prophet Nathan rightly rebuked him (2 Samuel 11:1-12:9). David's response though, recorded in Psalm 51, serves as an example for how we too should respond when we reflect on the sin in our lives. Not justifying or ignoring it but coming before God and acknowledging our actions.

At church it's easy for confession of sins to simply become a recital of words in bold, an attitude far removed from the model God desires of us (Ps 51:16-17). Instead, scripture advocates that we each regularly take time, wherever that may be, to reflect on where we have fallen short of God's standard in our own lives. Not because our eternal destiny or status as beloved children of God are at risk. Nothing can change those things. But because of the damage sin causes in our lives and to our relationship with God. For example, sin can bring a guilt that causes our prayer life to suffer as we avoid spending time with him. Similarly, by believing that we've failed him, we can start to question how (or even why) he loves us, developing a sense that we're unworthy of serving him. Thoughts such as these aren't grounded in truth, but the enemy will use anything to affect our relationship with God.

It's for these reasons that we're called to confess our sins. Therefore, perhaps spend some time reflecting on where you have sinned this past week before using the first 10 verses of Psalm 51 as a prayer of confession, knowing that God is faithful to forgive (1 John 1:9).

The Temple of Eden

Eden as a Temple

A temple is defined as the dwelling place of a deity and therefore Eden can be thought of as the first earthly temple of God. Eden is creation as God intended, him dwelling alongside humanity. It's a model ruined by the sin of Adam but one that will be reinstated upon the return of Jesus (Rev 21-22). The imagery of Eden is found in the tabernacle, and the Jerusalem temples whilst there are also numerous parallels between Eden and the future temple imagery found in Ezekiel and Revelation.

Adam as a Priest

If Eden is a temple then we can think of Adam as a priest. His tasks, to care and maintain the garden, are both Hebrew terms connected to the priestly roles of maintaining sacred space such as the tabernacle and later temples in Jerusalem. In post-exodus Israel (and a post-fall world) this was accomplished through the Levitical system of offerings that were unnecessary within the temple of Eden.

When we see Adam as a priest, we also understand why his actions have ramifications for all mankind. Just as Adam represented humanity, priests were appointed as representatives of the people before God meaning their actions had consequences which went beyond themselves (Lev 4:3). During the year, the priests bore the sins of the people before they were removed annually on the day of atonement, freeing the entire community from their sins. We do not bear the sin of Adam (Ezekiel 18), but we're still subject to the ramifications of his sin (Romans 5).

The Veil is Formed

As a result of their sin, Adam and Eve were cast from the presence of God. They were barred from the tree of life and therefore doomed to die (Gen 3:19). The Cherubim (angels) who guard it mirror the veil that is found in the later tabernacle and temples, separating the worshippers and priesthood from the presence of God within the Holy of Holies. This chapter is a launching point for the rest of scripture which proceeds to record how the curse of Eden was undone through God's interactions with Israel and the ministry of Jesus. When he died upon the cross, this veil was torn in two from top to bottom (heaven to earth). His death broke the curse of sin and the separation between man and God that existed throughout the Old Testament.

3. Abraham

Genesis 11:1-9, Genesis 12:1-7, Genesis 15:1-21

(Genesis 12:8 – 13:18, Genesis 16:1 – 17:27)

Trust in the Lord with all your heart and do not lean on your own understanding. In all your ways acknowledge Him, and He will make your paths straight. (Proverbs 3:5-6).

The Tower of Babel is likely to have been a ziggurat, a stepped tower common in ancient Mesopotamia which at the top had a room. No one would enter this room, for it was not intended for man, but rather it was built for a god. The tower reached up to heaven, enticing a deity to come down and reside in this room whilst at the base was an area for the community to worship in.

The people of Babel are building a tower to link heaven and earth, thus, among other things, fixing the separation caused by the sin of Adam. However, they were unable to fix this problem. It was something they would never be able to fix, irrespective of how high a tower they built. The problem could only be addressed by God who, as an act of grace, sets into motion his plan of restoration in the next chapter. Through Abraham, God would bring into being a nation, from the nation God would bring forth the Messiah, and in the life of the Messiah God would defeat the powers of sin and death forever.

In our modern culture we have inconsistent views on asking for help. It's often thought of as a sign of failure and so, like the people of Babel, we make a habit of trying to fix our problems in our own strength. We don't want to bother anyone else unless things have *really* gone wrong, at which point, we may sheepishly approach them. Yet at the same time, each of us also recognise areas where we have absolutely no ability to address our problems. If you were locked out of your house, it's unlikely you would try to pick the lock yourself, but instead would call an expert in to help.

It's this humble attitude that we should seek to apply to the whole of our lives; recognising our weaknesses and therefore relying upon God in all things instead of trying to do it ourselves and asking him as a last resort. God, in his love, will still respond to our prayers of desperation, but why delay? We worship a God who wants to be involved in all aspects of our lives and we would therefore be foolish to ignore him.

The Abrahamic Covenant

The Abrahamic Covenant describes a series of promises which God makes with Abraham over the course of his life. They address his own present issues, and the future that awaits his descendants.

Genesis 12:1-3

This short passage contains a series of promises that are expanded upon in subsequent chapters. In short, these promises were that Abraham would have descendants who would become a great nation (Israel), and that would be blessed with land (the Promised Land), and spiritual status (as God's chosen nation who entered into a covenant with him. The final promise given, that God would bless the world through Abraham's descendants, is the key lens through which to view the mission of Israel in the Old Testament - to draw surrounding nations to God through their example and witness of God's work among them. As Christians, we believe this mission to be fulfilled through the work of Jesus.

Genesis 15

Despite the earlier promises of God, Abraham still had no son and therefore failed to see how God's promises could be fulfilled. In this chapter, God reassured him that those things would indeed come to pass, focusing first on his descendants and then the land which had been promised to them. The promises were confirmed by the establishment of a covenant. When two parties agreed to enter a covenant, they would arrange animal parts and then both pass between them to indicate their mutual agreement. Casting Abraham into a deep sleep, only God moved between the animal parts meaning there were no conditions Abraham was obliged to keep.

Chapter 17

At this point Abraham was still without a son and so, once again, God reassured him of the promises he had been given. The chapter then proceeds to introduce the ritual of circumcision, something required of every male descendant of Abraham in order to signify their identity as members of Israel. The New Testament makes clear that as Christians we've entered into a new covenant with God that doesn't require this form of identification (Acts 15:1-29).

4. Isaac

Beer Roi = well of
Lahai God who sees me

Genesis 16:1-16, Genesis 18:1-15, Genesis 21:1-13

(Genesis 22:1 – 22:18)

Why do we have the Bible? Firstly, it's a record of God's historical interactions with Israel and the individuals who, though all flawed, accomplished great things by God working through them. The Bible also provides us with guidance for living in line with God's intentions, informing our actions and the priorities we should have. The primary function of the Bible though is to reveal God to us: who he is, what he's like and, ultimately, why we should follow him.

Scripture reveals many characteristics of God to us. If we were to rank them by significance, loving would probably be top of the list for most people, likely followed by some of the attributes we tend to focus upon: forgiving, holy, powerful, etc. One which should absolutely be a part of this conversation though is his faithfulness. Although we often think of faithfulness in terms of how we should remain faithful to God, scripture repeatedly affirms *his faithfulness* towards us. It's precisely because he is faithful that we can trust him to be merciful towards us, forgive our sins and forever show love towards us.

When God lists the ways in which he will bless Abraham, the majority would be fulfilled many centuries later. However, the promise that he and Sarah would have a child was one for the present. Years they waited before eventually, in a time of doubt, they took matters into their own hands. Abraham had the child he wanted, but with Hagar instead (Gen 16). When Sarah hears God repeating his promises (Gen 18) she bursts out laughing. How could a woman of her age give birth? We might expect God to respond with fury towards this lack of faith but that's not what happens. Instead God blesses Ishmael and Hagar and upholds his original promise to Sarah who subsequently gives birth to Isaac.

A theme repeated throughout scripture is the faithlessness of man compared to the faithfulness of God. As we will see, Israel continually failed to follow God, yet despite their actions he remained faithful to the promises he had made to Abraham. The same is true in our own lives. Whenever we doubt God, he remains faithful, because his faithfulness isn't dependent on us and what we do, but rather it's an unchangeable element of his character. He will never leave us nor forsake us and his love towards us will never cease.

The Call to Trust a Faithful God

As mentioned during this book's introduction, the Bible is made up of over sixty books, written by different authors and incorporating a variety of literary styles. However, despite this variety, there are a number of unifying themes which connect these different pieces to form one large, tapestry. The presence of God, the battle against sin, the anticipated Messiah and the idolatry of mankind are a few such themes, but perhaps the biggest is the call to trust in God. Even in the books of wisdom, which are more removed from the main biblical narrative, there is the implication that the words God speaks through them are ones we should follow, even if they're at odds with the world.

Trusting God goes far beyond merely trusting that he exists. Instead, what God desires from us is to trust in his character and the words he speaks. It's a form of trust that Israel, surrounded by a world who could not comprehend such belief, regularly failed to exhibit, but one that she was continually instructed to pursue. A trust that *knows* when we strike the rock it will bring forth water - not because we've done anything special but because God has said it will happen (Ex 17:1-7).

Of course in order to trust anyone we must conclude from observation that they are worthy of our trust. God's trustworthiness is underpinned by his faithfulness. The faithfulness of God is a character trait not found in the pagan religions surrounding Israel. The gods of Egypt and other nations were unpredictable and impossible to rely upon, possessing the same moral flaws and desires found within their human worshippers. Conversely, the God of Israel reveals himself to be unchangeable and of a significantly higher moral standing than his people. He was someone who the people of Israel could trust wholeheartedly.

The faithfulness of God is the most important character trait of God taught by the Bible, as without it, we have no reason to trust any of the other things he reveals to us. God may love us today, but what about tomorrow? An unfaithful God means that we have no hope at all. Ultimately, we are commanded to believe in Jesus and are promised that he will forgive our sins, but these things are entirely reliant upon the will of God. Because scripture reveals God to be someone faithful to his promises, we *can know without doubt* that when we put our faith in him, our sins are indeed forgiven.

5. Jacob, Esau & The Stolen Blessing

Genesis 25:19-34, Genesis 27:1 – 28:5

(Genesis 24:1-67)

Growing up there were two days I looked forward to above all others – Christmas Day and my birthday. Both were occasions spent having fun with family and friends but, more importantly, they were the two times each year when I would receive the various gifts I wanted. Not rewards for something I had done, but gifts which flowed from the love others had towards me. At all points of our life, receiving a gift is a positive experience, but the joy that accompanies this moment can often be quite short-lived. We tend to quickly grow accustomed to the presence of a new gift and so, once the novelty has worn off, our minds turn to newer, more pressing needs. The same can also sadly be true of God's gifts to us.

In the passage above, our shock at Jacob's deception can overshadow Esau's actions. Being Isaac's first-born son, Esau was heir to the family inheritance – an inheritance that included the promises God had given to his grandfather Abraham: that a nation descended from him would inherit the land of Canaan and bless the world. We may feel sorry for Esau, but, as this account reveals, he had such a low opinion of these blessings, these gifts from God towards his family, that he sold them for a single meal! Only after making the transaction did he begin to appreciate their value.

Every breath that we take and therefore every good thing in our lives is a gift from God that is worthy of our thanksgiving. Therefore, a lesson from this passage must be to not allow our hearts to grow so cold towards God's blessings that we begin to think of them as nothing. A great habit to get into is finding one thing to thank God for each day. This may feel like more of a challenge in certain seasons of our life, but whatever's going on around us we still have a God who died for us so that we could enter into a relationship with him and be free of the curse of sin and death. Even if that's all we can muster let's seek to be people with an attitude of gratitude.

The Family Tree of Abraham

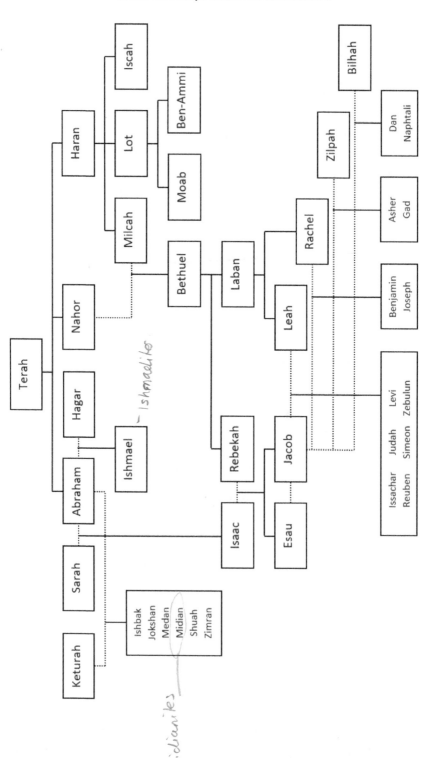

6. Jacob's Family

Genesis 29:1-35, Genesis 35:1-29

(Genesis 30:1-24, Genesis 32:3 – 33:15)

Having left his family to escape Esau, Jacob arrived at the house of Laban and met his two daughters. Rachel was a beautiful woman and as such demanded a high price from those who wished to marry her. However, before this could happen, Laban first needed to find someone willing to marry her elder sister Leah. The only description we're given of Leah is that she had weak eyes, however Laban's subsequent actions show that he saw trickery as the best way to ensure this happened. In her father's eyes, Leah was worth far less than her sister, a view that Jacob shared. However, unlike Rachel, she was able to bear him children. Desperate for Jacob to see her as he saw Rachel, Leah's recorded after each birth hoping that now, finally, Jacob would love her. But nothing changed. Jacob's heart was always set on Rachel.

The acceptance Leah desires, is something common in all of us. There's nothing wrong with wanting to be liked and we certainly shouldn't aim for people to hate us. However, like with most matters discussed in the Bible, the key is having a correct perspective. Worldly acceptance is untrustworthy and fleeting, relying upon the decisions and opinions of others and is therefore something that's ultimately outside our control. If we fail to recognise this, then we can become just like Leah, desperately striving and hoping that *this time* it will be different, and we'll receive the acceptance our heart longs for.

In contrast to worldly acceptance, the Bible reveals to us the acceptance we have in a God who will never fail us or let us down. Throughout the account of Jacob's family, it was he who accepted and loved Leah as she was, and upon giving birth to her fourth child, there's an indication that Leah's starting to understand this point for herself. Whatever our weaknesses, whatever our past, whatever our failings, whatever others think of us, God accepts us with an incomparable love.

Perhaps spend some time reading through the verses below, reflecting on the truths they declare and, through prayer, asking him to identify areas where you are craving acceptance instead of resting in the truth of who you are before him.

1 Peter 2:9   Psalm 139:13-16   1 John 3:1

Rom 5:7-8   Gal 2:20   2 Cor 12:9-10

Gen 35:1-29 more from prev
+ 3 more

Jacob = Israel

The Tribes of Israel

The twelve sons of Jacob (renamed as Israel) later become the heads of the "Twelve Tribes of Israel". The tribes are the foundation of Israelite social structure and are therefore mentioned in various lists which describe the nation. Confusingly, these lists often vary from one another due to the changing religious structure of Israel or (as is the case in Revelation) the theological point that the author wished to convey. However, a decent Bible commentary will generally explain the reasons for any differences. For the average person, the key things to understand about the tribes of Israel are their origin, the role of the Levites and the way that Israel was structured around tribal identity.

Old Testament

interesting

During most of the Old Testament, the people of Israel are politically (and geographically) organised according to their tribe: the son of Jacob from whom they descend. At the end of Genesis, Joseph's two sons are adopted by Jacob meaning they inherit their father's double portion of inheritance (Gen 48:22) and therefore become tribes in their own right. Later, the events of Mount Sinai see the Levites appointed to perform the priestly duties of the tabernacle and represent the people before God. These developments result in twelve tribes (10 sons of Jacob and 2 sons of Joseph) with the Levites functioning as an additional tribe.

When the Promised Land was divided, a portion was allocated to each tribe except the Levites. Instead, as God's appointed priests, their inheritance was the Lord (Deuteronomy 18:1-2). They were therefore spread throughout the land in order to best serve the people. Although each Israelite had a tribal identity, they remained united to one another through their shared identity as the covenantal people of God.

New Testament

Because of how the societal structure of Israel changed during the exile and period between the Old and New Testaments, the tribes are rarely mentioned in the latter. However, it's no coincidence that Jesus chose twelve disciples to follow him as through these twelve he established the church – a new elect group who are to worship and serve him. It's important to note, though, that the church hasn't replaced Israel. Nor have God's promises to Abraham and Israel been made obsolete. Such a belief is known as replacement theology and is not taught by scripture.

Ishmaelites – decendants Abrahams elder son Ishmael ⟩ see pg 30
Midianites – decendants of Midian a later son of Abraham nomadic tribes.

7. Joseph's Time in Egypt

according to Lion Handbook. interchangeable names characteristic

Genesis 37:1-36, Genesis 39:1-23, Genesis 41:1-45 of Near Eastern writing.

Joseph sold for 20 pieces of silver

(Genesis 40:1-23, Genesis 41:46-57)

Do you suffer with pride? If the answer is yes, then congratulations on your honesty. If the answer is no, then make sure you don't feel too proud about it. Pride can be an obstacle for each of us, particularly in the achievement driven culture we inhabit which from an early age encourages us to find value and boast in our accomplishments. If you ever watch an episode of the Apprentice, keep an eye on how the candidates constantly one-up one another, stealing sales, claiming credit for the work of others all so they can win the competition.

The account of Joseph illustrates someone who possessed a different mindset. Someone who learned to recognise that all his works were only possible because of God. At the beginning of the story he seems to be almost gloating about how special he is, yet what follows are a series of events where he's in the control of others. His brothers, the traders, Potiphar, the prison chief and finally Pharaoh. Standing before Pharaoh Joseph finally had the opportunity to have something good happen to him. To just stand up and say "Yes *I am* able to interpret these dreams and *I should* be placed in charge". Yet Joseph takes none of the credit. Instead, he points the praises of Pharaoh towards God, the real source of the interpretation. Similarly, he instructs Pharaoh to install a "discerning and wise" man over Egypt (41:33) whoever that may be. Joseph recognised his total dependence on God, and we should strive to act likewise, understanding that all of our talents ultimately flow from God, and that therefore all our successes are his too.

Acting with such counter-cultural humility is the kind of action that may also draw others to God. In today's passage we are shown the effects that Joseph's character has on those around him. In the presence of both Potiphar and Pharaoh, they each see something in Joseph that set him apart. They were able to discern the power of God working through him to such a degree that they entrusted their respective kingdoms to him. When thinking of how we can evangelise to those around us, we tend to focus on what we can say in order to convince them that Christianity is worth exploring. However, our actions can speak far more about God and his effect on our lives than words ever could.

God Speaks

I called to my god, but he did not show his face, I prayed to my goddess, but she did not raise her head.

I instructed my land to keep the god's rites and provoked my people to value the goddess's name. I made praise for the king like a god's, and taught the populace reverence for the palace. I wish I knew that these things were pleasing to one's god.

Who knows the will of the gods in heaven? ... Where have mortals learnt the way of a god?

The lines above are taken from an ancient Mesopotamian poem known as The Poem of the Righteous Sufferer and are included to demonstrate how distant people in the ancient world felt they were from the gods. The worshipper does all sorts of things yet has no idea if they are pleasing or upsetting to his god. The ancient gods weren't revelatory in the same way as the God of Israel who, through the Law, provided his people with detailed descriptions of what he expected of them. We worship a God who both spoke to his people then and who still speaks to us today.

Sometimes it's obvious that God is speaking to us, other times it's slightly less so. Therefore, whenever we hear his voice, we should seek to weigh what we've heard with what we already know about God as revealed in scripture. He is the same yesterday, today and forever, and so we can be certain that a word belittling us or instructing us to act contrary to his values isn't from God. Similarly, sometimes a person may give us a word they believe God wants to speak to us, but which makes no sense when we hear it. God may over time reveal what he was saying, but it may also be that the person was innocently mistaken.

Super-Natural Phenomena

Our God is one of miracles and therefore he has and is still able to reveal himself in super-natural ways. Examples from the Bible include his appearance as a burning bush to Moses (Ex 3:2) and the transfiguration (Matt 17:1-13) where the glory of Jesus was made visible to several of his disciples, fully revealing him to be God incarnate. Something else to be aware of is that the angel of the Lord, in the Old Testament, is synonymous with God himself and is thought by some to be a representation of Jesus. If this is the case, then whenever someone encountered this person, they were encountering God himself.

* reference

Dreams and Vision

In the accounts of both Joseph and Daniel, God spoke to different people through dreams and visions. This form of communication is found elsewhere in scripture and remains a common way that God speaks to us today. For example, there are many stories of Muslims who turned to Jesus after encountering him in a dream. The visions people in the Bible received were given in a way that either the recipient or someone close by could understand, and therefore we should expect the words God speaks today to be similarly intelligible.

Through Creation

Writing to the Roman church, Paul reminds his audience how creation itself testifies to its creator (Rom 1:20). "The heavens are telling of the glory of God", writes the psalmist (Psalm 19:1), something that's just as true now as when it was first written. Among other things, creation reminds us of the power, beauty and provision of God, as well as our God given responsibility to maintain it in line with his commands.

Through Others

God doesn't always speak to us directly. In the Old Testament God often spoke to the Israelites through one of their leaders or prophets and therefore he may likewise choose to speak to us through someone else. This method of communication not only encourages the recipient but can also enhance the faith of the person entrusted with delivering the message. Although we aren't hearing from God directly, him speaking through someone else certainly doesn't remove the authority of those words or diminish their significance.

The Voice of God

One of the most common ways for God to speak is through a voice that we alone hear. This may involve hearing an audible voice like the one Samuel heard (1 Sam 3), but often God speaks through our thoughts, bringing to mind certain things. When I was looking for a new job several years ago, I suddenly had the thought to apply somewhere I had never even considered. 24 hours later I had been given a job. It's again right to weigh what we think is the voice of God with what we know about him through scripture, but over time this process becomes easier as we learn to distinguish his voice from our own.

Experience

Although there's a risk that we begin to attribute every single thing to divine intervention, it's indisputable that God speaks to us through what we experience. When we seek guidance, he may open doors to an opportunity we never would have expected or prevent us obtaining something we were pursuing. In either case it can take great faith to trust what God is saying. God can speak through any circumstance: times of mourning can teach us of God's comfort; in times of want we can witness his provision. In all seasons of life God can speak to us.

Scripture

The Bible is God's revelation to us. The prophets record the words that God spoke to the nation of Israel, whilst in the New Testament the gospels demonstrate the priorities and teachings of Jesus. When we read these books, we have a window through which we can see the heart of God. That our worship should be focused on him alone, that we should treat our neighbour with love and that we should turn from sin and obediently follow him are just some of the messages God spoke, thus emphasising their importance to him.

All scripture however is God-breathed and therefore God can speak to us through any and all passages. Each verse may have been written for a specific purpose, yet the power of scripture is that it can speak to us in ways which transcend those original intentions. For example, Jesus's calming of the storm demonstrates his power over creation, and yet in reading this passage God may speak to us about a situation in our lives, reminding us that he's greater than any storm we're currently facing. That he is with us in the 'boat of life'.

The Holy Spirit

Underpinning each way in which we hear God speak, is the Holy Spirit who dwells within us. He convicts us when we do wrong, guides us through life and teaches us the ways of God. It is he who causes passages of scripture we have encountered dozens of times to speak to us in new ways. He doesn't speak to us because of anything we've done but because of who God is and his desire to be in relationship with us.

8. Jacob and Family Arrive in Egypt

Genesis 42:1-2, Genesis 45:1 – 46:7, Matthew 18:21-35

(Genesis 41:46-57, Genesis 42:3 – 44:34)

The Lord's Prayer has been used by believers throughout the world for thousands of years. Contained within are praises to God, a petition for him to act in our world and requests that he provide for us materially and spiritually. However, despite its short length, we might prefer it to be slightly shorter. "Forgive us our sins" is something we can all sign up to; but the requirement that we forgive others perhaps less so.

Forgiveness isn't something that always comes easily. A need to forgive means then we have been wronged, perhaps greatly or without there being a way for the situation to be rectified. It can also be that the person who has upset us doesn't even acknowledge their wrongdoing. In this passage, Joseph comes face to face with his brothers who had sold him into slavery and rejected him as a member of their family. We might expect Joseph to have seized this opportunity to gain revenge, however, this isn't what happens. Instead, Joseph shows them mercy, exhibiting the type of forgiveness God desires in our own lives (Matt 18:22).

The parable of the unforgiving servant illustrates how we should view this topic. The servant is rightly admonished for his lack of forgiveness, but something that always strikes me is that the amount he's owed isn't insignificant, he's been considerably wronged. He's not owed just a few pence but 100 denarii, around a third of a year's salary. Why is he rebuked so sharply then? Because the amount *he owes* would today be the equivalent of around four billion Pounds! However great the wrong we need to forgive, it's far less than what we've already been forgiven by God. It's from this perspective that our forgiveness should flow.

Knowing why we should forgive doesn't necessarily make it any easier, but it can at least remind us of the position that we want to ultimately reach. A piece of advice I once heard was that if we presently can't bring ourselves to forgive someone, that we instead pray that God would forgive them and, in time, bring us to our own place of forgiveness. It's amazing how freeing this can be in practice. A bitter, unforgiving heart leads to nothing but more pain, harming ourselves far more than those who have wronged us. Perhaps spend some time reflecting on whether there's anyone you need to forgive, asking for God's forgiveness towards that person and that he would enable you to let go of any anger.

The Nations of the Old Testament

The Old Testament assumes that the reader knows about the local geo-political situation. The following pages give some brief details about the major nations descending from Abraham and those surrounding Israel.

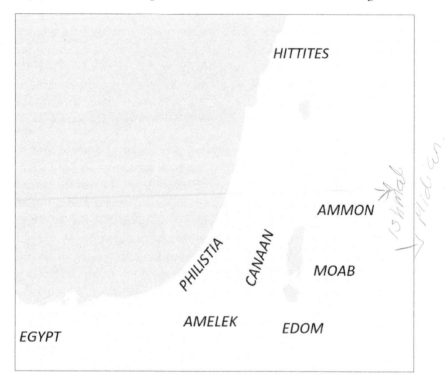

Israelites

The Israelites were descended from Jacob, who was renamed Israel, and whose 12 sons form the basis of the twelve tribes of Israel. They are God's chosen nation who entered into a covenant with him at Mt Sinai after their rescue from Egypt. For most of the Old Testament narrative the Israelites are located in Canaan and so subsequent references to the geographical location of Israel should be interpreted accordingly.

Ishmaelites

Descended from Ishmael, Abraham's first-born son, the Ishmaelites dwelt to the east of the map above where the main narrative of the Bible takes place and therefore don't appear frequently outside of the book of Genesis. Jewish and Islamic tradition would claim that the Arabic peoples are descended from Ishmael's twelve sons.

Midianites

Descended from Abraham's son Midian, the Midianites lived in an area a significant distance east of Israel and therefore, like the Ishmaelites, do not appear frequently in the Bible. They did however attack Israel during the time of the Judges before being defeated by Gideon (Judges 6-8). As they were from a similar location relative to Israel, the terms Midianite and Ishmaelite can be used interchangeably (Judges 8:22-26).

Canaanites

Canaan (and Canaanite) can refer to the various tribes descended from Ham's son Canaan (Gen 10:6-19), the geographical region where these tribes lived, or a particular group of people within this region. The gods of the Canaanite people included Baal and Asherah whom the Israelites were frequently guilty of worshipping. They were the primary inhabitants of the Promised Land before the Israelites arrived.

Edomites

The Edomites were descended from Esau (Jacob's brother) and so due to this relationship the Israelites were prohibited from hating them (Deut 23:7). However, Edom's desire to conquer Israel meant that several wars were still fought. When Jerusalem was captured (2 Kings 24-25), the Edomites fought alongside the invading Babylonians, an act that may have led to Obadiah's prophecy of destruction towards them.

Amalekites

The Amalekites were descended from Amalek, a grandson of Esau, but were considered distinct from the Edomites. They regularly fought against the Israelites either by themselves or alongside other nations and so were condemned to destruction by God (Deut 25:17-19). This didn't happen immediately, but over time, and with each successive defeat in battle against the Israelites, the nation slowly became less powerful.

Moabites

Descended from Lot's son Moab, the Moabites engaged in various conflicts with Israel until they were defeated by David. Ruth was a Moabite and serves as an example from the Old Testament that following God wasn't something available exclusively to the Israelites.

Ammonites

Descended from Lot's son Ben-Ammi, the Ammonites were another frequent adversary of Israel until their subjugation under Saul and David. However, once the Kingdom of Israel split, conflict resumed. Their god Molech is frequently condemned in scripture as his worship involved the sacrifice of babies by burning them alive (passing them through the fire), something that the Israelites too wrongfully carried out at times (2 Kings 21:6).

Philistines

The Philistines were another frequent adversary of the Israelites living in five city states to the south-west of Israel and who, although subdued by David, were only defeated for good during the time of Hezekiah. The Philistines appear at numerous times throughout Judges and 1 and 2 Samuel, most notably during the accounts of Samson, David and when they stole the Ark of The Covenant from Israel.

Egypt

Egypt is one of the oldest civilizations in the world and the first great empire that influenced the geographical setting of the Bible. It was the location that Jacob's family moved to during a famine and the place that their descendants were kept as slaves. After being rescued by God and led to the Promised Land by Moses, Israel's next interactions with Egypt came during the times of the kings. Throughout the whole narrative of the Old Testament, Egypt remained a powerful independent nation that played a role in various conflicts that took place.

Hittites

The Hittites are descended from Heth, the son of Canaan, and lived in an area north of Israel that stretched to the east of modern-day Turkey. Although they are listed as a tribe whom Israel needed to conquer in taking possession of the Promised Land, there aren't many conflicts recorded between them and in fact at times they were known to fight alongside Israel. They remained in existence throughout the Old Testament narrative but were no longer referred to as an independent nation during the time of Jesus. This was likely due to the different empires (Persian, Greek, Seleucid, Roman) who ruled the region in the time between the Old and New Testaments.

9. Moses Called to Lead the Israelites

Exodus 3:1-17, Exodus 4:1-17, Exodus 7:7-24

(Exodus 3:18-22, Exodus 5:1 – 6:13, Exodus 6:28 – 7:6)

How can I do this? The reaction of Moses when called to lead his people out of Egypt is one that will be familiar to many of us. A feeling of inadequacy compared to what we expect God requires. This perception will be considered at a later point, but something else that stands out in this passage is the way that God addresses these concerns of Moses.

When Moses says that no one will believe him, God doesn't argue but instead provides signs to be performed and the words that Moses should speak. Then, once Moses has complained that he can't speak well, God again doesn't correct him, but provides someone to speak on his behalf. Alone, Moses was incapable of rescuing the Israelites, but he was never alone. Instead, his ministry was defined by the continual presence and provision of a God who supplied everything necessary for Moses to serve him, and to sustain the people of Israel. Time (Ex 14) and again (Ex 16) the Israelites were faced with impossible obstacles (Ex 17), but on each occasion God came through for them.

The accounts from Exodus listed above describe the people moving from one crisis to the next without ever seeming to learn that they can trust God's provision. This can sadly be true in our own lives too. It's far easier to focus on the obstacle before us than remember the obstacles God has already overcome. We can therefore regularly feel a heightened sense of dread concerning the immediate future. However, the Bible teaches us that our God is the same yesterday, today and forever (Heb 13:8), and therefore just as he provided for the Israelites three and a half thousand years ago, he is able to provide for us. This is one of the key reasons that the history of Israel was recorded for future generations. So that they may lean on God's past provision when confronting their present needs.

For us, the Bible remains effective in this process, but something else that you may find helpful is keeping a prayer journal to record the ways in which God has answered you. Then, once an obstacle presents itself, we can use it to quickly recall what he has previously accomplished, trusting that the God who provided for us yesterday is still able to provide today.

Theory could be linked to Santorini eruption 1620 - 1600 BCE
see time.com/5561441/passover-10-plagues - real-history

Egyptian.
Egyptian
Plagues

water →
blood.

frogs

lice

flies

livestock
pestilence

boils

hail

locusts

darkness

death of
1st born

The Plagues of Egypt

The plagues of Egypt weren't random punishments that God caused to fall upon the Egyptians. They were instead a demonstration of God's power (7:5, 12:12). The plagues attacked objects that bore resemblance to the Egyptian gods (cattle, frogs), affected areas of life which the gods were supposed to protect (the harvest, health), or directly challenged individual gods such as the sun and Pharaoh himself. For example, the Nile turned to blood whilst Pharaoh was immersed in the river – a sacred rite connected to his claim of divinity.

As discussed previously (p14), the polytheistic worldview of people in the ancient world makes it highly unlikely that Egyptians would have denied the existence of Israel's God - why else does Pharaoh ask Moses to pray that the disasters cease (Ex 8:8,25). However, they would have certainly viewed him *God* as less powerful than their own gods. The plagues served to challenge this belief by showing God's power over the Egyptian deities and Pharaoh.

Most of the Egyptian gods had several spheres of influence and therefore although it may be possible to link each plague to one specific god, it's better to consider the plagues as challenging their collective power. A selection of Egyptian gods are listed below alongside some of their roles:

Hapi	God of the Nile Flood
Ra	God of the Sun
Haqet	Goddess of Fertility (represented by a frog faced woman)
Wadjet	Protector of Egypt
Seth	God of chaos and storms
Isis	Goddess of Medicine
Osiris	God of Agriculture and Vegetation
Horus	God of the Sun and Protection
Hathor	Goddess of Protection (one of many deities whose appearance was linked to cattle)
Pharaoh	Thought to be both a god and an intermediary between the people and the other gods

10. The Exodus

Exodus 11:1 – 12:51

(Exodus 7:25 – 10:29, Exodus 14:1-31)

When reading the Bible over recent years, I've increasingly been struck by the small details we often overlook. We can read a passage over and over and then suddenly something jumps out, perhaps a single word, that we never noticed before.

Consider God's instructions before the tenth plague. The Israelites are warned of what God intends to do, and told that to be protected, they must kill a lamb (or goat) and paint the animal's blood above their door. To an agricultural community such as Israel this wasn't too taxing of a request as there would have been many old, sick animals that could have served this purpose. However, they couldn't give just any animal - it needed to be perfect (Ex 12:5). With just one word, what was required of them became that much more costly. This theme of offering God our best is one found elsewhere in scripture. For example, in the book of Malachi, whilst addressing the dismissive, inconvenienced attitudes the people were harbouring towards worship, a direct message was delivered to them - how can you possibly give to God such pathetic offerings (1:6-14, 3:6-12).

It's easy to think of giving to God as a solely financial exercise, but our giving should go far beyond that. We're called to offer our talents, our time, our whole lives in worship and service to him. Even attending church on a Sunday is a form of offering, as we put him before other pursuits. Ultimately, whatever we give to God, even our time, is simply returning what he has given to us. What we're able to give will vary from person to person, but God is concerned with our hearts, not quantities. Jesus didn't compliment the widow in the temple for the amount she gave, but for giving all she had. For giving her best to God however insignificant it appeared to others (Mark 12:41-44).

In response I would encourage you to spend an hour this week with God in place of something you would usually never miss. Or perhaps more scarily, have someone who knows you choose what you give up! During this time, maybe reflect on what you currently give to God and whether anything should change in this regard. Whatever we're able to give to him, we should be guided by the knowledge that he's worthy of our best, not just the stuff we have left over.

Israelite Festivals

You shall observe the Feast of Unleavened Bread ... You shall celebrate the Feast of Weeks, that is, the first fruits of the wheat harvest, and the Feast of Ingathering at the turn of the year. Three times a year all your males are to appear before the Lord God, the God of Israel. (Ex 34:18, 22-23).

After leaving Egypt, the Israelites were given instructions concerning seven different festivals (feasts) that were to take place during the year. Although each had an appointed time of celebration, the Jewish calendar was based on the lunar cycle and therefore none of the festivals correspond to a specific date in our modern calendars. This is why Easter is celebrated on a different day each year. The three festivals mentioned in the above verses were occasions where all Jewish men were expected to journey to Jerusalem, and therefore Jesus's different visits to the city were centred on these dates.

Passover and The Feast of Unleavened Bread (Lev 23:4-8)

On the 14th day of Nisan (Mar – Apr) the people celebrated Passover and immediately following this was the seven-day Feast of Unleavened Bread. This was a time of celebration and remembrance of Israel's deliverance from Egypt which culminated in the first Passover. Unleavened bread was eaten because of God's instruction to the people for them to prepare bread without yeast (Ex 12:8), allowing them to prepare the meal more quickly. It may also be linked to reminding the people that they were to live lives worthy of their rescue (1 Cor 5:6-8).

Firstfruits and The Feast of Weeks (Pentecost) (Lev 23:9-22)

The day after the first Sabbath following Passover was the presentation of firstfruits. Offerings from the beginning of the barley harvest were provided, indicative of God's provision which the people trusted would be reflected in an abundant future harvest yield. It was on this day that Jesus was raised from the dead, the firstfruits of many (1 Cor 15:20).

Fifty days later the Feast of Weeks was celebrated, a day also known as Pentecost as the Greek for fiftieth was pentekoste. It was also one of the three festivals mentioned above that Jewish males were expected to observe in Jerusalem. During the celebration, the book of Ruth was read to the people and offerings were made from the beginning of the wheat harvest, again representing the people's faith in God's provision.

The Feast of Trumpets, Day of Atonement and Feast of Tabernacles (Lev 23:23-43 and Lev 16)

All three of these festivals were celebrated during the seventh month of the Jewish calendar (Sep-Oct). On the first day of the month was the Feast of Trumpets. Described as a day of memorial it likely paralleled the trumpet blasts which accompanied God's appearance to the Israelites at Mt Sinai (Ex 19:16,19) and the establishment of the Old Covenant.

On the tenth day of the month was the Day of Atonement (Yom Kippur). This was a day of fasting rather than celebration where the sins of the people from the previous year were dealt with. The passage in Leviticus 23 gives guidelines for how the people should act during the day whilst Leviticus 16 outlines the rituals which the priests needed to perform. It was the only day of the year where the High Priest was permitted to enter the Holy of Holies, and he did so in order to sprinkle the blood of a sacrificial bull upon the mercy seat of the Ark of The Covenant (p50). Following this, a male goat would have the sins of the people placed upon him and be driven out from the community. Although it wasn't required, someone would typically follow the goat and kill it to prevent the spiritual conundrum which would have arisen if the goat, and therefore the people's sins, had returned to them.

Finally, beginning on the 15th day of the month and lasting for seven days, was the Feast of Tabernacles (also known as the Feast of Booths or the Feast of Ingathering). During this festival, the people would build and sleep within small shelters (booths). Constructed with branches, they were intended to represent the living conditions that their ancestors endured in the wilderness, reminding the people of their nation's history. Offerings made during this festival would have come from the products gathered at the beginning of the Autumn harvest.

When Jeroboam built the golden calves at Bethel and Dan to dissuade his citizens from worshipping in Jerusalem (1 Kings 12:25-32), he established a festival on the 15th day of the eighth month. This may well have been an attempt to replicate the Feast of Tabernacles that would have taken place exactly one month prior. If this was the case, then verse 33 is emphasising the fact that his festival wasn't ordained by God but was a product of Jeroboam's own intentions.

11. Israel at Mt Sinai

Exodus 19:1 – 20:17, Exodus 24:1-28

(Exodus 21:1 – 23:33)

Our God is one of rescue. The Bible records him rescuing both entire nations and seemingly insignificant individuals from their problems. Of course, what may seem insignificant to us can be of great significance to God, in this case demonstrated through the love he has towards nations and individuals and the importance he places on them.

When God brought the Israelites out of Egypt, they had yet to agree to any sort of covenant relationship with him. Therefore, upon reaching Sinai each person was free to walk away. It may have been a foolish decision, but it remained a decision they were able to make. However, stay or leave, they had still been liberated: freed from a life of slavery. God's rescue stemmed not from what the people could offer him, but from his love for them, and his faithfulness to the promises he had made centuries prior to Abraham.

The same is true of the gospel, the greatest rescue of all. We are never capable of living a perfect life and are therefore on the path to death. Yet God stepped into this situation and rescued the world through his death upon the cross. By believing in him and not ourselves, we are forgiven and welcomed into the family of God. We are fully reliant upon the saving work of Jesus and because of the love he has for us, this gift is freely offered to all. Not everyone accepts this gift, in fact most reject it, but the gift is still there for them should they choose it.

Throughout the Bible a cycle emerges of people rejecting God, falling into suffering and requiring rescue from God. Through his love towards them he does this over and over again. However, even knowing this, many of us can at times feel uncomfortable approaching him in prayer, particularly when we are seeking help for the same thing multiples times or when we are responsible for our predicament. What we need to remember in these situations is that Jesus has already died for the many, many ways we will each fail him. The Bible continually demonstrates that God's love and faithfulness do not depend on what we offer him, but on who he is.

The Old (Sinaitic) Covenant

Most references to a covenant in the prophets (or the Old Covenant in the New Testament) are describing the covenant God made with Israel at Mt Sinai. It takes the form of a Suzerain-Vassal covenant, something seen most clearly in the layout of Deuteronomy which specifies the laws to be obeyed and the blessings or curses which will accompany the people's adherence to these laws. It was never intended to last forever and has now been replaced by a newer and better covenant inaugurated through the ministry of Jesus.

Stipulations (Deuteronomy 6 - 27)

Deuteronomy is largely made up of regulations governing how the people should live alongside one another and their responsibilities to God. Many laws are repeating instructions that have already been given in the previous three books which is a reason why the book gained its name (Deuteronomy translates as second law in Greek). Along with Lev 19:18, the heart of this law is given in Deut 6:4-5, "Hear, O Israel! The Lord is our God, the Lord is one! You shall love the Lord your God with all your heart and with all your soul and with all your might."

Blessings and Curses (Deuteronomy 28:1-68)

If the people adhered to the above stipulations, then God would greatly bless them. He would establish them as a nation (v1,9) and allow them to take ownership of the land they had been promised (v11). They would no longer be slaves but would be set above the nations (v1,13). Every aspect of their lives would be blessed (v6). The people, livestock and the land would produce offspring (v4,11) and lead to great material blessings for the nation (v12). They would be an example to the world of what happens to those who diligently follow the Lord (v10).

The text then proceeds to list a range of curses which will fall upon the people if they are unfaithful to the covenant. They stand in contrast to the above blessings (v6,19) and so a lot of the imagery is repeated. Rain shall not fall, and the ground will become as iron (v23-24) preventing an abundant harvest. They would be defeated by their enemies (v25). Their children would be conquered by foreign nations (v49), uprooted from the land they were given (v63) and be scattered throughout the world (v64, 2 Kings 17 and 25). They would be an example to the world of what happens to those who fail to follow the Lord (v37,46).

The Holiness of God

Throughout the Bible, God is regularly described as holy. The word appears over 200 times in the opening five books of the Bible and is also prevalent within the prophecies found in Ezekiel and Revelation. Holy is the term that best describes God but is often poorly understood.

Holiness Defined

A common belief is that holiness refers to the moral perfection of God. Although God is indeed without sin and the term is at times used to denote this aspect of his person, this definition conveys only a small part of what it means to be holy. Instead, the word is best defined as describing something that is set apart. God's moral perfection is indeed set apart the rest of creation, but his distinctiveness far exceeds just this characteristic. God being described as holy conveys how he transcends creation and, as such, emphasises how he is uniquely worthy of worship. Objects set apart for service to God are also described as holy. For example, Israel and the church were both identified as holy nations, the tabernacle was comprised of a holy and most holy place, etc.

A Wholly Holy God

God is described not just as holy, but as holy, holy, holy (Rev 4:8). His holiness isn't a single character trait but encompasses everything about him. He loves us with a holy love, a love unlike that of anyone else. He administers holy justice and responds to sin and injustice with a holy anger. His person and character are fully set apart from all others.

The Call to be Holy

Throughout the Torah (the first five books of the Old Testament), the Israelites are called to be holy in light of God's holiness. This instruction includes a moral dimension but isn't a command to be perfect. Instead, it's a call for them to be distinct from the pagan nations and worship God alone. Many of the laws, particularly those which seem peculiar to us, are teaching principles that set the Israelites apart. Prohibited from performing fertility rituals, or worshipping multiple gods, the people of Israel were called to be dedicated to God in a way unlike any of the surrounding peoples.

12. Construction of the Tabernacle

Exodus 25:1-40, Exodus 26:31-37, Exodus 40:17-38

(Exodus 26:1-30, Exodus 40:1-16)

Once the Israelites agreed to enter a covenant with God, their means of fellowship with him were dramatically altered. The account of creation, in the first several chapters of Genesis, reveals God's original intention to dwell alongside mankind. However, as a result of their sin, Adam and Eve were cast from his presence and a barrier was erected between us and God. The tabernacle and sacrificial system which accompanied the covenant were designed to circumvent this divide. Therefore, although a barrier still existed (the veil which separated the Holy of Holies from the Holy Place), the tabernacle was how God made his dwelling place among the people again.

We worship a God of relationship, who desires to be involved in our lives. Therefore, the question for each of us is whether we want that. Outside of mandatory offerings there remained a decision for each Israelite concerning how involved they wanted God to be in their lives. They could just give what they had to, or they could offer numerous offerings to God about all things. The peace offering was an opportunity for the worshipper to eat a meal in the house of God (p53), a privilege not afforded to their ancestors. But it was a voluntary offering. There was no weekly time set aside or obligation to participate, it was, instead, an opportunity that they could choose to either enjoy or ignore.

The same dynamic is at work within our own lives. Through the work of Jesus, we no longer need to kill animals to enter God's presence; we're forever free to approach him. But when and how we do this remains our decision. On the one hand, we can choose to confine him to our worship on a Sunday morning and spend the rest of the week by ourselves. Alternatively, we can choose to invite him into all areas of our lives, praying continually (1 Thess 5:17) about all things (Phil 4:6).

Genuine relationship can only come through choice, never through compulsion. God's offer of relationship is thus built on us being willing participants. His desire, as with the Israelites, is to make his dwelling in our life, and to be involved in everything we do, but he will never force himself upon us. The decision is ours to make. What will you choose?

The Tabernacle, Priesthood and Sacrificial System

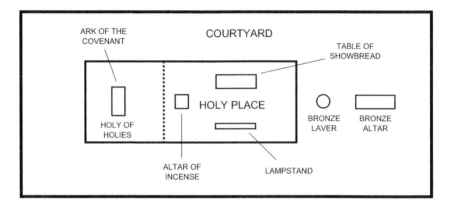

The Tabernacle

The tabernacle was divided into three sections: the courtyard, the Holy Place and the Holy of Holies (the Most Holy Place) where God dwelt. All Israelites were allowed into the courtyard and priests could enter the Holy Place, however, only the High Priest was permitted to enter the Holy of Holies - once a year on the Day of Atonement.

Altar of Incense

This altar wasn't used for sacrifices but was instead used to continually burn incense. The fragrant cloud would fill the tabernacle and rise to the heavens symbolising the prayers of the people rising to God. Each year, on the day of atonement, the altar would be purified through the blood of the sacrificed bull and goat.

Ark of The Covenant

This was a chest that contained the tablets of the Ten Commandments, the rod of Aaron (Num 17:1-18:7) and a pot of manna. The cover was made of pure gold and had two cherubim facing one another. The space between was called the mercy seat and was where the High Priest would sprinkle blood during the Day of Atonement to bring forgiveness to the people. When Jesus is described as the propitiation for our sins (Rom 3:25, 1 John 2:2) it's using the same root word as used for the mercy seat. His death upon the cross accomplished forever what needed to be renewed annually in Israel.

Bronze Altar

Located in the courtyard this would have been the first item an Israelite saw upon entering the tabernacle - an instant reminder of their sins and separation from God. The daily burnt offerings were placed upon here, as were the burnt elements of the other sacrifices. The fire that they were placed within was started by God and thus was never extinguished.

Bronze Laver

The laver was where the priests would wash their hands before offering sacrifices or entering the Holy Place. We no longer have to adhere to the purity laws of ancient Israel, however through baptism we too are symbolically washed clean.

Menorah (Lampstand)

The Menorah was fashioned out of pure gold and provided light for the Holy Place. Seven cups shaped in the form of almond flowers held the oil which burned, a design that may have been chosen due to the speed with which almond flowers bloomed after winter, thus reminding the people of God's speed to answer their prayers. Another of the titles Jesus gave himself was the Light of the World. This was a reference to both the Menorah and God's manifestation as the pillar of fire which guided the nation as they journeyed through the wilderness.

Table of Showbread

On this table twelves loaves of bread were displayed, representing the provision of God towards the twelve tribes of Israel (the nation as a whole). During his ministry, Jesus declared that he is the bread of life, the ultimate provider in whom we will never want for anything.

The Veil

The veil was a curtain several inches thick that separated the Holy of Holies from the Holy Place. Through Adam's sin, mankind had been separated from God, and although the tabernacle brought people closer to him there was still a need to keep a division between a Holy God and a sinful people. As Jesus died on the cross, the temple veil was torn showing that the barrier between us and God has been removed. We are now free to approach God without the need for animal sacrifice.

The Priesthood

The priests were a group appointed by God to serve the tabernacle and oversee Israel's religious activities. Every priest was a male from the tribe of Levi, however, that doesn't mean that every male Levite was a priest. The Levites didn't receive a portion of the Promised Land (Num 18:20) as they were scattered throughout Israel in order to serve the people. This also fulfilled the prophecy given to Levi by his father Jacob (Gen 49:7). The priests were intermediaries between the people and God, bearing their sins and representing them before him. Alongside their religious roles, priests were appointed to judge legal disputes and were responsible for teaching the law to their fellow Israelites.

Offerings (Sacrifices)

Leviticus can be thought of as an instruction manual regarding how the Israelites were to worship God. Contained within are guidelines for five types of offering, each with a particular purpose and subtle differences in terms of what was offered, the processes involved, and who (if anyone) ate the offering. Something consistent across all the offerings was the partial burning of what was given whilst all but the grain offering involved an animal being killed and having its blood spread.

The burnt offering (Lev 1) was offered for the atonement of sin. It was performed in the period before the covenant was established and so was an offering that the people would have been accustomed to prior to the events of Sinai. The priests made this offering twice a day on behalf of the people, but individuals could also make it for themselves. Typically, a male herd animal was sacrificed but for poorer worshippers, pigeons and doves were permitted instead.

The grain offering (Lev 2) was offered as a sign of thankfulness for what God had done and, as with the burnt offering, was also performed before the covenant was given. The term grain offering is based on what was typically offered, however the original Hebrew is better translated as a tribute offering, something that also conveys more accurately the heart of the ritual. What was offered wasn't just what the worshipper gathered from creation but those gathered items transformed through labour. Therefore, before being offered, olives were turned into oil, wheat into flour, etc. This requirement reminded the worshipper of both God's provision and their own responsibility to govern and make use of what God had given them. Part of the offering was burnt, rising with a prior burnt offering, whilst the rest was consumed by the priests.

The next three offerings all originate from the covenant given upon Mt Sinai. The peace offering (Lev 3) was a voluntary act of worship and was unique in that whilst still requiring the sacrifice and burning of an animal, the worshipper was able to participate in a meal within the tabernacle, eating the portion that wasn't due the priests. The creation of this offering highlights the significance of what occurred through the giving of the covenant and God making the tabernacle his dwelling place. Through this offering the worshipper was now able to eat and have fellowship with God in a way that had never been possible before.

The sin offering (Lev 4) was offered as a way of maintaining the purity of the tabernacle and the worshipper. It atoned for unintentional sin that the people committed, even those that hadn't been identified. Priests typically ate the portion not burnt and, through this, bore the sins of the people. This process culminated with the annual day of atonement. On that day, the High Priest would make atonement for the sins of the entire nation through sin offerings, burnt offerings and the use of a scapegoat, purifying the tabernacle and priesthood from all sin. As with the burnt offering, the animal killed was based on who was making the offering with specific provisions made for worshippers who were unable to afford a flock animal. When Jesus entered the temple and saw people selling pigeons, he was angered not by the items being sold, but by the market culture. The sale of birds was supposed to enable poor worshippers to make offerings to God, however the actions of the temple authorities were preventing this from occurring.

The final offering described is the trespass or guilt offering (Lev 5) which was given to make atonement for unintentional sins that resulted in a loss of property. The regulations surrounding this offering were much like those of the sin offering as they shared a similar purpose, however an additional requirement was that the worshipper provided financial restitution to the person(s) who had been afflicted. Through this, the individual reconciled themselves to both God and neighbour.

13. Forty Years in the Wilderness

Numbers 13:1-2, Numbers 13:25 – 14:45

(Numbers 11:1-35, Numbers 13:3-24)

It's remarkable to read the accounts of Israel's journey to the Promised Land and the challenges they faced. Despite all that God had done to rescue them from slavery in Egypt, the people regularly descended into a panic, assuming that all hope is lost. This passage sees their doubts come to a head. When Moses sends spies into the Promised Land the majority return with tales of horror! "How can we possibly defeat the Canaanites?" they ask, demanding to return to Egypt. Their lack of faith in a God who has already repeatedly rescued them can strike us as inexplicable. However, the reason behind this isn't that they doubted the existence of God, but that they simply didn't trust him.

The call to trust or believe in God is perhaps the most common across the whole Bible, but this goes beyond just acknowledging his existence. Instead, it's communicating God's desire that we trust him with our whole lives, both now and into the future. This isn't something that's necessarily easy or even a choice that's ours to make. Trust needs to be earned and due to the pain and wrongdoing we encounter, most of us will find it hard to trust those we don't know. So what can we do?

In order to trust people, we need to know that they're worthy of trust – people who won't betray us or cause us deliberate harm. When we get married, we have no guarantee, other than their word, that our spouse will be faithful. However, over the course of a relationship that sort of trust is built, or otherwise, by our partner's actions. It's for this reason that it's so important to regularly spend time with God. How can we trust him if we don't know him? And how can we know him without spending time with him through prayer and reading the Bible?

The Bible records God's interactions with the world. However, more important than most of the events described, are what those events reveal to us about God. It's not overly important to us today that Joseph was sold into slavery in Egypt and rose to become governor. What's more important is what that story shows us about God's presence with us amid persecution, and his ability to work terrible situations for good. As such, we should endeavour to make use of the opportunities afforded to us and resolve to know God deeper day by day.

The Journey to the Promised Land

Although the journey from Egypt to the Promised Land takes forty years, the events recorded in the Bible mostly take place at either end of this period. This layout is outlined in more detail below.

The First Year (Ex 16 – Num 14)

The events recorded in this section all take place within a year of leaving Egypt. Most of the text is concerned with the Sinaitic covenant, but another key theme is God's provision. For example, in times of need, he miraculously supplied the Israelites with manna, water (Ex 16-17) and quail (Num 11). At the end of this period, Moses sent spies into Canaan. Their reports caused the people to respond with terror, leading to the next and longest portion of the journey...

The Wilderness Wanderings (Num 15-19)

As punishment for their continual lack of faith, the people were prohibited from entering the Promised Land (Num 14:26-35). Instead they were sentenced to wandering in the wilderness for the next forty years. Few events are recorded during this time but the censuses at either end show how the nation changed (Num 1 and 26).

Approaching the Promised Land (Num 20-Deut 34)

This final section of narrative describes the end of the people's time in the wilderness and their path to the edge of the Promised Land. Key events that take place include the deaths of Aaron and Miriam (Num 20) and the blessing given to Israel by Balaam (Num 22-24). The section concludes with Joshua's appointment as leader of Israel (Deut 31) and the death of Moses (Deut 34).

The last few chapters of Deuteronomy record some of the final words Moses spoke to the people and the choice they had to make (Deut 30:11-20). If they adhered to the covenant, then they would inherit life and national prosperity. However, if they turned from God and instead worshipped the gods of the surrounding nations, it would bring death and destruction. The rest of the Old Testament narrative should be read with this passage in mind. It's the choice that defines what happens to each successive generation and is a choice that we too are called to make today as we either follow the ways of God or our own desires.

14. Conquering the Promised Land

Joshua 3:1-17, Joshua 6:1-25 √

(Joshua 2:1-24, Joshua 10:29 – 11:23)

Having entered the Promised Land, the Israelites are faced with their first real challenge: the city of Jericho. Fortunately, God has a plan. Instead of building catapults and battering rams to destroy the walls of Jericho, the people of Israel are instead told to walk around the city blowing trumpets. I guess it's unexpected, but I can't imagine the inhabitants of Jericho being particularly impressed or concerned by this strategy. As a soldier in the Israelite army it could well have felt pretty humiliating.

There are many instructions in the Bible that on the surface seem a little strange. When Moses was leading the Israelites a generation earlier, he was instructed to strike a rock with his staff to bring forth water (Ex 17:5-6). When Elisha raised the widow's son to life (2 Kings 4:32-37) he did so by lying on top of him! Imagine if hospitals scrapped CPR in favour of that approach. There are of course reasons for these commands that go beyond the present crisis. God didn't need them to walk around a wall in order for him to tear it down, it was instead a demonstration that the Israelites could and should trust him. It's the most important lesson they could learn but one they generally struggled to accept.

Although we may think it unlikely that we'll be asked to perform these sorts of actions, there will still be occasions where God leads us in ways that we struggle to understand. Being turned down for a job that we were sure he had lined up for us. Being led to a location that we would never have chosen ourselves. However, as with our examples from the Bible, we are called to trust whatever God has spoken, assured that as we follow his instruction, he will not lead us astray.

Reading this, you may have been reminded of something God has spoken to you which you haven't yet acted upon, perhaps because it seemed confusing or scary. If this is the case, spend some time in prayer asking God to give you the boldness and faith required to obediently follow his words. We interpret things from our own vantage point, but God sees everything. He knows us better than we know ourselves and so, whatever we think we know, he most certainly knows best.

Understanding the Conquest

The accounts of Joshua and Judges include some of the more difficult passages of scripture to reconcile with a loving, merciful God. However, there are several facts we should consider when trying to understand this period of Israelite history.

Purpose of Historical Literature

When we read the conquest accounts, we tend to think of them as contemporary history, focusing on specific details and attempting to construct an image in our mind of exactly what took place. However, historical accounts in the Bible are far more focused on what the events recorded reveal about God. Therefore, the primary intention behind Joshua including Israel's victories over her enemies, is to teach the reader about the provision and faithfulness of God, their need to be obedient to the covenant and their calling as the people of God.

Hyperbole (Exaggeration)

Another key difference between ancient and contemporary history is how they avoid (or make use of) hyperbole. If we were asked to record an ancient battle, we would likely focus on the order of events, the different strategies deployed and the number of fatalities with the intention that our account was as accurate as possible. By contrast, ancient accounts of conquest are full of hyperbole. In chapter 10, Joshua is said to have "struck all the land", "left no survivors" and "utterly destroyed all who breathed". However, the book of Judges condemns the Israelites for *not* defeating the Canaanites completely, something that's also apparent when reading the second half of Joshua.

A challenge for us as modern readers is to understand what the use of hyperbole does and doesn't mean. For example, although we need to take care with how we interpret specific details, it certainly doesn't indicate that the events reported never took place. As previously discussed, the purpose of historical literature in the Bible is to teach future readers about God. If the events the author wants us to base our understanding of God's faithfulness on never took place, then it ceases to be evidence worth recording. The God presented in the Bible is drastically different than the pagan gods around them and therefore in order to accept this radical new god the people need good reason to do so. Fabricating stories and miracles won't help with this aim.

58

The Wickedness of the Canaanites

The Canaanites are presented in scripture as an evil people who engaged in a variety of sexual and spiritual sins including child sacrifice. Although they weren't expected to conform to the regulations set out in the Sinaitic Covenant, their actions violated a morality which God expects of all people (Romans 1). The Bible is clear that although God is merciful, he is also just, administering punishment on various nations. Other examples of God's judgement on groups of people are recorded in the prophecies of Habakkuk and Obadiah.

The Purity of Israel and Methods of Conquest

As the people of God, Israel's purity was paramount, and therefore it was necessary to remove a wicked culture that risked compromising the moral standards God desired of them. There were several ways in which this could be carried out. For example, both Rahab and Ruth (a Canaanite and Moabite) were individuals welcomed into the nation of Israel and we have no reason to think that these were unique occurrences. Similarly, despite deceiving the Israelites, the Gibeonites were allowed to co-exist with Israel (Joshua 9).

Various Canaanite groups chose to fight, thus making battle necessary. However, we can't conclude that this was how Israel treated every tribe they encountered. The Book of Joshua condenses years of history into several pages of text and therefore it clearly does not record every single interaction between the Israelites and Canaanites. Again, this isn't the primary purpose of historical literature in the Bible.

We Trust in God's Character

However, even with these considerations, it's impossible to avoid the fact that over this time many battles were fought, and thus many people were killed. As humans we often strive to understand every little detail but sometimes God's ways are beyond our understanding (Romans 11:33-34). In this life we will never know exactly what occurred during the conquest of Canaan. How many and who were killed? Whether they were given a chance to repent? Ultimately, though, in these situations, we trust in God. A God who administers justice but who does so fairly. A God who has the right to give and take life as he sees fit, but who equally has the right to determine the eternal state of those killed.

15. The Period of Judges

Joshua 24:1 – 24:28, Judges 2:11-23

(Joshua 23:1-16, Judges 1:1 – 2:10)

Growing up, our environment has a massive impact on us. I hate cats because each cat I saw as a child used to scratch me. I love sport because my family always watched sport. I will always ask for a slice of Victoria sponge if it's available because my mum bakes the best Victoria sponge in the world!

Our environments play a pivotal role in the beliefs and interests that we hold, and it's because of this influence, that God commanded Israel to continue driving the Canaanites from the Promised Land. The Israelites were being asked to reject a polytheistic worldview, and worship God alone - instructions that ran contrary to the world around them, and that would therefore be far harder to follow if surrounded by a people who served numerous gods at the same time and saw nothing wrong in doing so. If you're trying to give up cake, then it's probably unwise to take a job in a bakery where the staff eat the leftovers at the end of the day. However, the people failed to obey God's instructions regarding the Canaanites and therefore, as God knew would happen, the people began to imitate their sinful practices. The Book of Judges records God repeatedly having to rescue his people because of the afflictions brought about by their sins.

Just as Israel was instructed to do, we should each seek to place ourselves in an environment that is conducive to a strong relationship with God. If our job conflicts with the values and teaching of Jesus, then it might be best to leave. If our friends are encouraging us to engage in sinful activities, then it might be best to spend less time with them. There does of course need to be a balance. If we hide from the world then the world will never change; our friends will be less likely to hear about Jesus for example. The point here isn't about running away, but simply being wise. Our relationship with God should be the most important thing in our lives and therefore we shouldn't ignore things that affect this relationship. If we find ourselves regularly falling into sin based on who we spend time with or what we're watching and listening to, then it's right that we reflect on whether they're helpful. As Paul says to the Corinthians "All things are lawful, but not all things are profitable. All things are lawful, but not all things edify" (1 Cor 10:23).

Not about prohibitions but whether it is a good idea.

The Era of Judges

From the time of Joshua until the establishment of the monarchy, Israel had no overarching political establishment. Instead, each tribe was instructed to continue conquering their portion of the Promised Land. They were self-governing yet remained united through their shared identity as God's chosen people.

During times of oppression, God raised up judges who, anointed with the Spirit, were to lead his people. Although some of them may have exerted influence over the whole nation, they were often responding to local challenges and consequently their rule may have been confined to a specific region. If this is the case, then it's likely that the judgeship of certain individuals overlapped, making it hard to precisely date the events they were involved in.

Unlike kings, judges were appointed and empowered by God, and therefore judgeship wasn't necessarily a hereditary position. They were his chosen servants but, as with all of God's people, none of them were perfect. Therefore, although there's much to be gained by studying their lives and what God accomplished through them, none are intended to be role models that we should fully imitate.

The Record of Judges

Most of this period in Israel's history is recorded in the book of Judges. Just beforehand, in the final chapters of Joshua, the people chose to renew the covenant, promising that they would adhere to its regulations and accept the consequences brought upon by unfaithfulness. Judges records Israel's repeated failure to live up to this promise and their resulting sufferings. It was a time where the people continually rebelled against the rule of God and turned, instead, to the gods worshipped by the surrounding pagan nations (Judges 2:11-19). A time where everyone did what was right in their own eyes (Judges 21:25).

The book consists of six cycles of rebellion (chapters 3-16)[1] which each follow the same pattern. First, the people engage in idolatry and worship false gods. As a result, destruction is brought down upon them and they cry out to God for help. In their time of need, God appoints judges to lead them, and through the power of God, the people overcome their adversaries before the cycle begins all over.

[1] The final five chapters record events outside of this cyclic narrative and therefore don't necessarily occur after the judgeship of Samson.

Six Cycles of Oppression

First (3:7-11)

Oppressors – King Cushan Rishathaim (most likely a Canaanite ruler)

Judges – Othniel[1]

Second (3:12-31)

Oppressors – King Eglon of Moab (allied with Ammon and Amalek)

Judges – Ehud[1], Shamgar

Third (4:1 – 5:31)

Oppressors – King Jabin of Canaan

Judges – Deborah[1]

Fourth (6:1 – 8:32)

Oppressors – Midian and Amalek

Judges – Gideon[1], Abimelech[2], Tola, Jair

Fifth (10:6 – 12:15)

Oppressors – Ammon and the Philistines.

Judges – Jephthah[1], Ibzan, Elan, Abdon

Sixth (13:1 – 16:31)

Oppressors – The Philistines

Judges – Samson[1]

After the book of Judges, Israel was judged by Eli and Samuel. This period is described in the first few chapters of 1 Samuel.

[1] Primarily responsible for overcoming the oppression.
[2] Not typically considered a judge as he seized power for himself.

16. The Call for a King

1 Samuel 8:1-22, 1 Samuel 10:17-24, Ephesians 4:14-31

(1 Samuel 9:1 – 10:16)

In asking for Samuel to crown them a king, the rebellion of the Israelites reached a new low. Israel was established as a theocracy (a nation where all power flowed from God), a system vastly different to the monarchies in surrounding nations. A king in Israel wasn't prohibited (Deut 17:14-20), but what grieved God was that the people's request flowed from a desire to be like everyone else. They were rejecting not just his kingship and the way he had led them, but their identity as a distinct and holy nation (Ex 19:5-6). They chose to believe what their world said about human leadership instead of what God had spoken on the subject.

As the church, we're called as Israel were, to be distinct from those around us. A light to the world (Matt 5:13-16), no longer conforming to its ways, but instead being transformed by the renewing of our minds (Rom 12:2). However, just as in Israel, we too are surrounded by worldviews that conflict with the values God desires of us. Our culture is increasingly focused on the self, on a pursuit of happiness and satisfaction attained through relationships, sex, power, wealth, success and the opinion of others. Civil disagreement has been replaced by bitter and divisive arguments whilst a distinct lack of forgiveness sees lives ruined from ill-judged words spoken years prior. These and many other examples stand in direct contrast to a Bible that teaches us to put God and others first (Phil 2:3-4), that our identities are found in Christ (Gal 2:20) and that we should surrender our lives, hopes and desires, to him (Matt 16:24-25). That each person, however strongly we disagree with them, is still made in the image of God (Gen 1:26-27) and is therefore due our love and forgiveness (Eph 4:32).

The values of the world have a danger of shifting not just our perspective on certain social issues, but our relationship with God and how we view ourselves. We're designed to be in relationship with him and therefore worldly pursuits can never fill the Christ shaped hole at our centre. When we allow ourselves to be defined by our bank balance or seek satisfaction through relationships, we lose sight of our identity in Christ and the love of a God who accepts us as we are and who will never abandon us. We should each be careful to weigh what the world says with the words of scripture, not allowing the truths of who we are, who others are and who God is to become obscured.

Foreign (Pagan) Gods

Throughout their history the people of Israel engaged in the worship of various foreign gods. It's beyond the scope of this book to provide a detailed look at every different deity mentioned, however below are several summaries of the more influential pagan deities in Israel's history.

Baal

Baal is the god most synonymous with Israel's idolatry. Although Baal was a title given to various local gods (Num 25:3) it was also the name of an individual god in the Canaanite religion, son of the chief god El and his wife Asherah. Baal's spheres of influence included war, weather and fertility (human and agricultural), all elements which appealed to a small, agricultural nation such as Israel. His worship involved temple prostitution, sexual sins and child sacrifice.

Asherah

Asherah was a Canaanite fertility goddess, the wife of the chief god El, and another key figure in the idolatry of Israel. Worship of Asherah was centred on Asherah poles which, although not described in detail, were likely sacred wooden poles or trees and are regularly mentioned in the accounts of 1 and 2 Kings.

Molech

Molech may have been the name or title of a god, but in either case the term is describing an Ammonite deity whose worship was forbidden in Israel (Lev 20:1-5). As outlined in this passage, an element of his worship involved the sacrifice of babies by burning them alive (passing them through the fire), something that the Israelites too wrongfully carried out at times (2 Kings 21:6). It was thought that by offering your firstborn to Molech, he would bless your family.

Other Deities and Their Worshippers

Ashtoreth / Astarte (Consort of Baal) – Sidon / Canaan (1 Kings 11:5)

Chemosh - Moabites (Jeremiah 48:13)

Dagon – Philistines (Judges 16:23)

17. Saul as King

1 Samuel 13:1 – 14:45

(1 Samuel 11:12 – 12:25/1 Samuel 15:1-35)

The rejection of Saul as king can be a difficult passage to understand. He is shown to be disobedient yes, but God's penalty can appear harsh, particularly when Saul appears remorseful. However, some knowledge of Old Testament culture illuminates some of Saul's bigger flaws.

When a pagan king marched into battle is was important that he had the support of his gods and that they felt no anger towards him. Religious rituals such as sacrifice provided a way for the gods to be kept happy and when we look closely, we see that Saul shares these same attitudes. He saw God as a tool to be used and therefore rather than obeying the instructions of Samuel, he decided that to be victorious in battle he needed to intervene and give something to please God (13:9-12) or impress him through fasting (14:24). As king of Israel, Saul was supposed to be an example of how people should worship God, but it is clear through these texts that Saul lacked the sort of faith God desired.

His attempts to please God also demonstrate Saul's lack of understanding concerning God's grace – a concept that's explored in more detail on the following page. God could be trusted to defend Israel (a nation which came into being through the grace that God showed Abraham), not because of any action that Saul took, but because of who he was and the promises he had made towards them.

God's grace is seen throughout scripture and culminates in the ministry of Jesus. His death, the death of an innocent man, brings life to us all, and therefore despite each living sinful lives deserving of punishment, we're able to be welcomed into God's family and receive eternal life through faith in him. This message of grace is radically counter-cultural. We're used to earning rewards through good work, not having them bestowed upon us without reason, meaning that it's incredibly easy for us to think as Saul did. To believe that we need to behave a certain way or do certain things in order to receive (or not lose) God's love. Such an attitude can be exhausting. However hard we try we'll never be able to attain the perfection that we think God expects. Fortunately, the message of the Bible is one of recognising our weaknesses and resting on the promises and love of God. It's by doing this that we can enter the rest that Jesus promises to all who come to him (Matt 11:28).

The Grace of God + Mercy

For people outside of church circles, grace is probably most associated with the prayer given before eating a meal. However, the term is best understood as being linked to an undeserved blessing. If you were to walk up to a stranger and give them an envelope full of money, then that would be a gift of grace. They have done nothing to warrant such a gesture, it flows only from your own heart.

The grace of God is most clearly seen in the ministry and death of Jesus and is therefore a key point of emphasis for the New Testament writers. However, because of this, it can be easy to overlook that God's grace is displayed throughout the entire Bible. Following the creation of the world and the sin of Adam and Eve, God graciously provided them with clothing and set into motion a plan to redeem creation. As the Old Testament progresses, God's interactions with Israel continually testify to his grace. They were rescued from Egypt before agreeing to any form of covenantal relationship with him and were subsequently blessed with a sacrificial system through which they could enter God's presence and go deeper into relationship with him. Their conquering of the Promised Land wasn't down to anything they had done (Deut 9) but was a result of God's faithfulness to the promises he had made with Abraham – promises that likewise flowed from his grace. Then, through centuries of rebellion during the times of the Judges and Kings, God repeatedly rescued his people despite their actions violating their agreement with him.

As is the case with the example above, God's grace often goes beyond just giving an unearned gift, to bestowing a gift upon people who, through their actions, are more worthy of punishment than reward. The grace of God is therefore very closely linked to his mercy, where God relents from inflicting a punishment that someone deserves. This doesn't mean that justice and punishment never occur. As we have already seen (and will continue to see as we journey through the Bible) there's plenty of justice administered to Israel as a result of their sin. However, God's reprimand still flows from his grace and love, and therefore, alongside his justice, we see too his longsuffering and patience towards people who don't deserve it.

— Message of bible
recognise our weakness
rest in God's promised love.

18. David's Time in the Wilderness

1 Samuel 16:1-23, 1 Samuel 18:5 – 19:12, 1 Samuel 31:1-6, Psalm 57

(1 Samuel 23:7 – 24:22)

As Christians a key element of our worship is praising God in song and prayer. David was a man devoted to worshipping the Lord in this way, as demonstrated by the 75 psalms attributed to him. When the Ark of the Covenant was returned to Jerusalem, he's described as "leaping and dancing before the Lord", not caring for a moment about how foolish it made him look (2 Sam 6:12-23).

There's much that we can learn about worship through studying David, not least regarding what our motivations should be. Often our worship stems from what God has done for us and it's of course right that we praise him for these things. However, if this is our sole drive for worship, then how do we react when disappointment comes our way? When life is full of failure and pain? It's for this reason that our worship should instead be centred on the person of God. David wrote Psalm 57 whilst Saul was attempting to find and kill him, yet despite these circumstances it is filled with praise. "I will give thanks to You... I will sing praises to You", "Your lovingkindness is great to the heavens and Your truth to the clouds".

Although worship enables us to encounter God, the heart of worship isn't the worshipper, but who we worship. Whatever trials we may be facing God remains forever worthy of our praise. David experienced a great amount of pain in his life, pain that may resonate with us today. However, through it all, David's relationship with God and devotion to scripture meant that he was able to retain a view of God not defined by his suffering. A view that was impossible for David not to rejoice over. In all things God remains our faithful Saviour (Psalm 42) and rescuer (Psalm 54) whom we can trust (Psalm 55). A God who died for us in order that we could be reconciled to him (Romans 5) and whose love for us never fails. Praise the Lord!

The Psalms

The Book of Psalms is a collection of 150 songs and prayers written over the course of the Old Testament by a range of authors, which have been used by believers for thousands of years. When being collated they were grouped into five collections (books):

Book 1: Psalms 1-41

Book 2: Psalms 42-72

Book 3: Psalms 73-89

Book 4: Psalms 90-106

Book 5: Psalms 107-150

There's no scholarly consensus as to why they're grouped in this way. One theory is that they reflect and represent the five books of the Torah (Genesis – Deuteronomy). However, whatever the original intentions were, their grouping was certainly intentional, and therefore it's possible to identify common themes in each book.

Types of Psalms

The psalms are each unique in content and structure making it difficult to place them neatly into several pre-defined types. However, there are still certain broad styles that can be identified, some of which are listed below with examples:

Lament psalms (4, 44, 79) are individual or corporate expressions of sorrow. They outline a trial that the relevant person(s) are presently experiencing and often implore God to intervene.

Thanksgiving psalms (65, 118, 138) are individual or corporate expressions of thankfulness for God and what he's done in their lives.

Royal psalms (2, 101, 110) focus on God's role as King of Israel or on the human king's responsibilities and promises received from God.

Praise psalms (30, 95, 98) invite the reader to worship God, often focusing on several aspects of his character.

Wisdom psalms (37, 73, 127) provide advice for life and therefore read similarly to passages from Proverbs.

68

19. David as King

2 Samuel 6:12-23, 2 Samuel 8:1-18, Psalm 13

(2 Samuel 15:1-37, 2 Samuel 16:15 – 17:16, 2 Samuel 18:1-17)

In reading through the Bible, there's probably no-one outside of God himself that we come to know more deeply than David. This is because as well as being told what he did and said, we also hear what he thought. David is credited as the author of 75 psalms, and by studying these passages we gain a remarkable insight into the emotions David felt.

Their honesty provides a blueprint for what our prayer life should look like. We can come before God and pour out our hearts before him, even if we feel frustrated or angry (Psalm 42:9-10). Psalm 13 is one such psalm. David's life is fraught with opposition and times of trial such as when Saul was attempting to kill him, or his son Absalom rose up and tried to seize the throne. If through your own sufferings you've ever felt as though God was ignoring your cries for help, then the words of this psalm will likely resonate with you. I think we can all feel a degree of comfort that such a well-regarded character in the Bible had the same frustrations and doubts that we do.

So how should we react when God seems silent? We may, for whatever reason, just not be hearing his voice. It can be that we're dismissing what he's saying because we aren't willing to accept his words, or that he's choosing to speak through other people that we likewise overlook. I'm also guilty of praying for help without waiting to hear God's response. Prayer shouldn't be solely one-way traffic but rather it should involve times where we wait and listen for his voice.

At certain points though, God's silence is unexplainable. In these times it can be helpful to focus not on why we can't hear him, but on what his silence doesn't mean. God is someone who keeps his promises to a thousand generations (Deut 7:9), and therefore we can know that he hasn't abandoned us (Psalm 139:7-10) or stopped loving us (Psalm 100:5). He hasn't ceased to care for us (Psalm 23:1-6). Regardless of whether we can understand God's silence, we can be confident in the person of God and his love for us. Whatever we're feeling, we can know that he'll never leave us nor forsake us (Deut 31:6).

Suffering

The question of how a good God allows suffering is one that believers have wrestled with for thousands of years. We each experience pain and loss, and therefore it's unsurprising that the topic is also discussed at length by the people of the Bible. Below are some very brief answers that the Bible presents, however it's worth stating up front that even if we can formulate a coherent theology of suffering, we may still be unable to explain specific instances of suffering. In those times we're instead to trust in the person of God, remembering his faithfulness and presence with us whatever we are experiencing.

Human Caused Suffering and Free Will

A large amount of suffering isn't caused by God or nature, but by humanity. The Bible describes the sin of Adam as causing suffering and death, but even looking at the present, we can see how we're inherently sinful and guilty of inflicting enormous pain upon one another. Consider for example how global trade policies are designed to protect Western interests at the expense of others. How when we disagree with or hate one another, mankind has historically responded with conflict.

God could intervene in these situations, and at times he does, but to prohibit us from making these choices would be to deprive us of our freedom. God desires relationship with willing participants, not puppets, and therefore free will is a necessary consequence. God's judgement is dependent on us having agency and thus being responsible for what we do. We're also commissioned to spread his kingdom and bring his love to those who need it, actions that include confronting the injustices that plague our world, as the abolitionists did in the 18th and 19th centuries. If we choose not to do so then it seems hard to blame God for what our inaction has left unopposed.

Death

A lot of things considered 'evil' aren't evil of themselves but lead to bad outcomes. For example, earthquakes and hurricanes aren't evil, they're natural events that we perceive as evil because of the death and damage that result. Death is the one guarantee of life and is therefore something we will each confront. However, it has also been defeated upon the cross and consequently, although events which lead to death may cause us great sadness, we need not lose all hope (1 Cor 15:51–57).

Spiritual Warfare

Throughout the early church, believers faced a great deal of violent persecution, a situation which sadly remains the case for much of the global church. Jesus had warned his followers that this would happen. They weren't of this world and consequently the world hated them (John 15:19). God has chosen the church to preach the gospel and build his kingdom on the earth; therefore, it should be unsurprising that forces of evil oppose us. As humans, although we'll never fully understand the mechanisms of spiritual warfare, that's no reason to deny the reality that all followers of Jesus are engaged in a spiritual war. (Eph 6:10-18).

The Purposes of God

Suffering can also be allowed to afflict us due to the purposes of God, purposes that are likely beyond our comprehension. For example, suffering highlights the problem of sin in the world, leading both to an understanding that something needs fixing, and highlighting the contrasting goodness of God. On a personal level, what we inflict on others reminds us of our need for a Saviour, whilst what we see in the world should further motivate us to share the good news of Jesus.

Times of suffering can also deepen our relationship with God and are described by Paul as a means of growing in perseverance, character and hope (Rom 5:3-4). It's during trials, that we learn what it means to rely on God in a way that isn't possible in times of blessing. Although there's obvious value in reading that God loves us, is always with us, protects us, etc, it's through life, and particularly amidst pain and sadness, that we understand these statements are more than just words, but instead unchanging truths. Not opinions we've formed ourselves, but concrete facts about God that we can trust and confidently share with others.

A God who Will End Suffering

Although we're presently afflicted by all forms of suffering, the Bible is clear that God takes no pleasure in this. Isaiah 65 for example, describes a God who doesn't ignore or condone injustice and those inflicting pain upon others, but one who will deal with them justly. This message is one reflected too at the end of Revelation, with the promise of a future no longer filled with pain and death, but where those evils are no more (Rev 21:4). A future of hope that, due to the trustworthiness and faithfulness of God, we can be assured will come to pass.

20. The Davidic Covenant

2 Samuel 7:1-29, Isaiah 9:2-7, Jeremiah 23:1-8, 1 Kings 2:1-11

(2 Samuel 22:1-51, Isaiah 11:1-10, Psalm 110)

As David considers all that God has done for him, and the unglamorous nature of the Lord's dwelling place compared to his own palace, he is moved to rectify the situation by building him a temple in Jerusalem. Although the prophet Nathan at first encourages David's intentions, God quickly intervenes in a quite unexpected way. Rather than blessing these plans, God forbids David from proceeding any further (1 Chron 22:8) instead entrusting the task of construction to one of his descendants.

When we think of trusting God, we often focus on trusting him when our instincts are saying no, especially when we're scared or unsure of what God is asking us to do. However, what can be harder in practice, is trusting God when he catches us by surprise and tells us not to do something. Our heart may be set on an idea that makes complete sense to us or, as is the case with David here, that we see as being a way of serving God. Therefore, how can he possibly not want us to do it?

The reason we can trust God's "no" is exactly the same reason that we trust his "yes": because of who he is and his love for us. We may not understand why God is preventing us from doing something, but we can still trust that he has our own, and the church's, interests at heart. Ultimately this should give us a great sense of peace, whatever life throws our way. For example, when people are rejected from a job, they can be left unsure and anxious for the future. We too, may feel a degree of anxiety or even pain at this kind of rejection. However, as followers of Jesus, we can rest in the knowledge that a God who loves us is guiding our steps. Whenever God has closed a door in my life, he's had something in store which turned out to be far better than what I had planned.

We are called to surrender our lives to God (Matt 16:24-25, Romans 12:1), obeying him when we're led down roads we would rather avoid, *and* when we're prevented from going down those we're excited about. If you are facing major decisions over the coming weeks, pray that God would guide you according to his will, and that he would give you the faith to trust his guidance, whether expected or otherwise.

The Davidic Covenant

Corporately Unconditional

Like the Abrahamic Covenant, the covenant God makes with David includes unconditional elements relating to land, descendants and how God would bless both him and his family. The key promises given are that the Israelites would be granted a land safe from affliction, that there would always be the right to rule for David's descendants, and that one of his descendants would establish an everlasting kingdom. Although this agreement is described just after David has become king of Israel, the text indicates that it may have been given to David far later in his reign: once all Israel's enemies had been subdued (v1). Historical literature isn't always ordered chronologically, but rather theologically, and therefore this passage may have been placed here due to the return of the Ark of the Covenant in the preceding chapter.

Individually Conditional

If God promised David that he would have an everlasting dynasty, then how do we explain subsequent kings of Judah being removed from power, or the periods that Judah was ruled by foreigners? The promises made in the covenant concern an eternal right for a person from David's line to reign, but individually, that right was still dependent upon that person's faith and allegiance to God. In David's final words to Solomon (1 Kings 2:1-4) it's clear that neither David nor Solomon considered it permissible for him, or future descendants, to act as they pleased and violate the law of God. Ultimately what follows in the accounts of 1 and 2 Kings are a series of leaders who mostly followed the gods of the nearby pagan nations and were punished accordingly.

A Covenant of Hope

Despite the apostasy of Judah, the promises made to David were still unconditional. During times of exile and into the New Testament, the Israelites maintained a hope that a person from the line of David would rise up and once again rule as king over them: the Messiah. The gospels make it clear that the early Christians believed this promise had been fulfilled in the person of Jesus. Someone descended from David (Matt 1:6) and someone who through his death and resurrection now reigns over the earth (Phil 2:9-11) today and for all eternity (Rev 21-22).

21. Solomon Builds the Temple

1 Kings 6:1, 1 Kings 6:37-38, 1 Kings 8:1-66

(1 Kings 5:1 – 6:38, 1 Kings 7:48-51)

When Solomon addresses the people after the construction of God's temple, he begins and ends his prayer of dedication by reminding them of God's faithfulness to his promises. God's words spoken to David concerning who would build the temple had now been fulfilled and looking back at the previous centuries the people could see how the promises God made to Moses (and Abraham before him) had come to pass. He had rescued them from Egypt, given them an inheritance and blessed them greatly.

Reading the Bible, the narrative moves so quickly that it can appear as though these promises were being fulfilled immediately. However, that wasn't the case. From the time of Moses until the reign of David when the nation took ownership of the whole of the Promised Land, around 500 years passed. The temple also took decades to move from vision to reality. Another significant promise in the Old Testament concerns the arrival of the Messiah: a man from the line of David who would establish an everlasting kingdom. However, from the point at which God first promised this to David to the arrival of Jesus, nearly 1000 years passed.

Our society is increasingly obsessed with speed. Vast sums of money are spent on railways which shave 30 minutes off a journey time or upgrades to the internet in order that the page we want to read loads a fraction of a second quicker. Speed is a key measure of success in many parts of life and therefore it's easy for us to expect a good God to fulfil his promises immediately. When he doesn't, we can lose hope, believing that perhaps we were mistaken or that God has changed his mind.

In these moments, we can be comforted by passages of scripture such as those mentioned above, that reveal how we're not alone in waiting on the promises of God, but that in each case those promises *were fulfilled.* We may not be able to discern when or how God will act, but we can be assured that he will (1 Kings 8:56). Therefore, if God has promised something to you, or a community you're a part of, that you're still waiting for, be encouraged that a faithful God does not forget his promises.

Solomon's Temple

Overview

Solomon's Temple was the first temple to the Lord built in Jerusalem. Having been prevented from building the temple himself, David passed the project on to his son Solomon who began construction in the fourth year of his reign. Seven years later the building was complete, marking a spiritual high point for the nation as God, who had guided them thus far and defeated all their enemies, was finally able to dwell among his people in a house worthy of his name. It has also been theorised that the location chosen (Mt Moriah) was the mountain that Abraham brought Isaac to whilst in the same region (Gen 22:2).

Appearance and Functionality

Even if the temple was relatively small (90ft x 30ft and 45ft high) when compared to the (all be it much later) Temple of Artemis (380ft x 200ft and 60ft high), it would still have been the most impressive building a typical Israelite had seen. Apart from the visible presence of God that dwelt within (1 Kings 8:10-11), the most stunning aspect of the temple was its decoration. In just the Holy of Holies, 21 tons of gold were used and throughout the whole building there were hundreds of tons of precious metals and woods. The temple succeeded the tabernacle as the centre of Israel's worship, however functionally it remained the same. The temple was still divided into three parts, the same types of furniture were present, and the same religious rituals were performed.

Idolatry and Destruction

Following the reign of Solomon, the people of Israel descended into a life of idolatry, worshipping the gods of the surrounding pagan nations, and building numerous images and altars through which they could be served. At times, these were even placed within the temple.

As a result of these sins, the Babylonians conquered Jerusalem in 586BC - around 380 years after the temple had been constructed. The city walls and temple were destroyed whilst the treasures it contained (excluding the Ark of the Covenant) were taken to Babylon. There they remained until the exiled people were allowed to return and rebuild Jerusalem. This chapter of Israel's history will be explored more fully in subsequent readings.

22. Solomon as King

1 Kings 9:1-9, 1 Kings 11:1-43

(1 Kings 9:10 – 10:29)

[handwritten: if you walk faithfully ... and obey I will establish your royal throne over Israel for ever. v 4 & 5.]

But each one is tempted when he is carried away and enticed by his own lust. Then when lust has conceived, it gives birth to sin; and when sin is accomplished, it brings forth death. (James 1:14-15).

The rule of Solomon can be divided into two parts. For the first half of his reign, Solomon diligently followed the Lord, faithfully building the temple that his father David had first envisioned. He was blessed with extraordinary wisdom and is generally thought to have been the author of Song of Songs, most of Proverbs and perhaps Ecclesiastes. However, despite this positive start, Solomon's reign ultimately ended in disaster. Through the influence of his hundreds of wives, Solomon began to worship the gods of the neighbouring nations, descending ever deeper into a life of idolatry and sin far removed from God's intentions.

Solomon's life should serve as a warning to each of us regarding the destructive power of sin. As James explains above, from desire comes temptation, from temptation sin and from sin death. What starts as desire can, if left unchecked, become an all-consuming need. Small transgressions committed to meet this need, become ever larger until eventually we can even reach the same place as Solomon - consciously rejecting God's commands to follow our own path (11:9-11).

Sin can ultimately be enslaving, but even prior to this point, sin will always damage our relationship with God. Therefore, we should all be alert to its development in our lives and proactively seek to address it. For example, it may be wise to seek the support of others or actively avoid situations that are likely to see us stumble. We should also aim to identify the root cause of our sin. A love of money isn't a result of actually loving money, or even what it buys, but is more likely rooted in coveting what those purchases offer: happiness, security, a sense of accomplishment. These needs are typically things that only God can satisfy, as Solomon himself perhaps rediscovered later in his life (if he did write the book of Ecclesiastes). The key to any transformation is our lives though, is prayer and the work of the Holy Spirit. A Spirit that doesn't condemn, but that offers us love, forgiveness and restoration. A spirit that enables us to live in the freedom from sin that Christ won upon the cross (Romans 6:1-14). *[handwritten: things only God can supply]*

[handwritten: sin of loving money → buys → happiness, security, sence of accomplishment]

Why Solomon is Rejected

In Deuteronomy 17, God provides a list of commands concerning the conduct of any future king or leader of Israel. Falling into a life of sin, Solomon breaks all of these rules and consequently has the kingdom taken away from his family.

Military Might

he shall not multiply horses for himself, nor shall he cause the people to return to Egypt to multiply horses (Deut 17:16).

Now Solomon gathered chariots and horsemen; and he had 1,400 chariots and 12,000 horsemen … Solomon's import of horses was from Egypt and Kue (1 Kings 10:26,28).

Leaders of Israel were commanded not to build great armies. A large army was a sign that the leader was trusting in their own ability to defend the nation and therefore indicated that they doubted either the sincerity of God's promise to protect them or his ability to do so.

Marital Conduct

He shall not multiply wives for himself, or else his heart will turn away (Deut 17:17).

He had seven hundred wives, princesses, and three hundred concubines, and his wives turned his heart away. (1 Kings 11:3).

Leaders were to be loyal to God alone and were therefore forbidden from taking many wives. Solomon moving away from God is directly attributed to his wives and their worship of various pagan gods.

Accumulation of Wealth

nor shall he greatly increase silver and gold for himself (Deut 17:17).

Now the weight of gold which came in to Solomon in one year was 666 talents of gold … So King Solomon became greater than all the kings of the earth in riches (1 Kings 10:14,23).

Leaders were also forbidden from accumulating wealth. As well as demonstrating a lack of faith in God's provision, the unnecessary gathering of money can naturally cause financial hardship in others.

23. The Kingdom Splits

1 Kings 12:1-32

(1 Kings 15:1 – 16:34)

God has bestowed many blessings upon his followers, but the church is often overlooked as one of them. Attending can be considered an inconvenience or placed behind more 'important' priorities, whilst cynical mindsets can lead us to view our church solely in terms of its shortcomings. Also, as is the case with any blessing, over familiarity can cause us to lose sight of its significance, such as how much it sustains our spiritual wellbeing. That is until we find ourselves without one.

There's no such thing as a perfect church but focusing on negatives can obscure the immense value that they offer us. A church isn't merely somewhere to worship and learn about God, it's a place where we find ourselves surrounded by other believers, following a similar path to our own. With that comes the opportunity to lean on the wisdom of those who have come before us and lived through the same issues that we're now facing. For example, when I first attended University, I was greatly appreciative of the support I received from a friend who had started the same journey the previous year and was therefore able to speak wisdom into situations I was encountering.

Apart from simply approaching one another in times of need, one way in which this can be accomplished is by following the biblical principle of mentoring. The relationships between Jesus and his disciples, Paul and Timothy, and Elijah and Elisha are just several such examples. It may be something else that needs to be crammed into an already busy life, but the benefits can be enormous.

Perhaps spend some time this week considering who you have in your life who can support you with spiritual and practical advice. Is there someone who you could approach to be a spiritual mentor, or could you instead offer to meet with someone else and mentor them? Inheriting a fragile kingdom Rehoboam sought advice from two groups, his friends and the more experienced national advisers. Although he chose to listen to the short-sighted advice of his friends, the elders spoke wisdom that, had it been followed, may have preserved the nation of Israel, and prevented the suffering that befell them. Our journey through life will likewise be filled with challenging times and decisions. We would be wise to make use of the wisdom God has placed around us.

Empires

Throughout the rest of the Old Testament narrative, Mesopotamian history is defined by three Empires: Assyrian, Babylonian and Persian. Each empire plays a significant role in the history of Israel, particularly around the periods of exile.

The Assyrian Empire (911BC – 609BC)

The Assyrians were the first of these empires and were a constant threat to the Northern Kingdom of Israel. In 720BC they managed to conquer the nation, enslaving the inhabitants and transporting them across their empire. However, despite attempting to do so, they were unable to defeat the Southern Kingdom of Judah. The last twenty years of the Assyrian Empire were marked by civil wars that led to their eventual defeat by a Babylonian led force and the destruction of Nineveh.

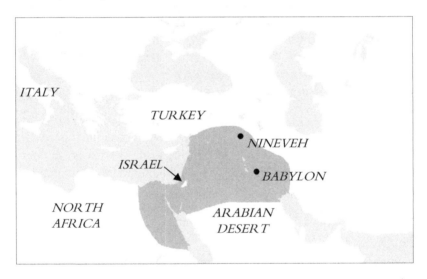

(Modern names have been used for all locations apart from Nineveh and Babylon)

The Babylonian Empire (626BC – 539BC)

The Babylonians governed a similar area to the Assyrians but managed to also conquer Judah, destroying the city of Jerusalem and exiling its inhabitants to Babylon (2 Kings 25). Daniel and Ezekiel are both written to this group of exiles, with Daniel in particular providing a glimpse of what life in Babylon looked like. In 549BC Cyrus the Great revolted from Babylonian rule, eventually defeating them ten years later (2 Chr 36:22-23). Babylon thus became a province of the Persian Empire.

The Persian Empire (550BC – 330BC)

The Persian Empire grew to be far larger than either the Assyrian or Babylonian empires before them. Their king Cyrus was responsible for allowing the exiled Israelites to return to their land and rebuild Jerusalem, however the nation remained under Persian rule for the next two-hundred years. This task and the roles that the Persian kings played are recorded in Ezra, Nehemiah and Esther. The Persian Empire ended with the expansion of the Macedonian Empire (often known as the Greek Empire) led by Alexander the Great.

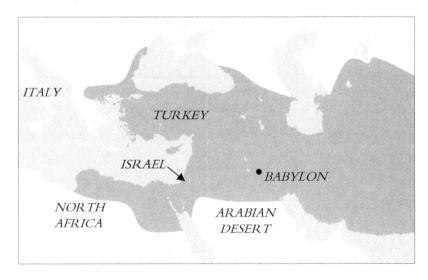

24. The Idolatry of Israel

1 Kings 22:1-40

(1 Kings 18:1 – 19:21, 1 Kings 21:1-29)

To be a prophet in the Ancient Near East was a dangerous job. Before a king took military action, it was customary for him to seek affirmation from prophets who could determine the will of the gods. However, in these situations the prophet faced a dilemma. The king was generally considered to be somewhat divine, or at least in his position of authority because the gods willed it. Therefore, a word spoken against the king's plans could be taken as an attack on not just their idea but their right to rule. Angering a king was an action that didn't usually end well. When Micaiah was approached for advice, he had two choices. Lie and please the king (22:6) or tell the truth and risk his fury (v17-23). As a genuine prophet of the Lord, he chose the latter and was subsequently thrown into jail. However, as the rest of the chapter shows, his words were true and the king was killed in the ensuing battle.

There can be great risk attached to speaking truth into certain situations or taking a stand on issues of injustice. If we're at work and see our boss treating someone poorly then there can be both a professional and financial cost associated with confronting that behaviour. If people around us are behaving wrongly then again there may be a cost to standing up for what's right. However, this is the model Jesus, the prophets and the apostles each followed, and one we're called to emulate (Eph 5:11). When Jesus saw what was going on in the temple, he drove the merchants from it (Matt 21:12-17). When Paul saw Peter treating Jews and Gentiles differently, he confronted him (Gal 2:11-14) and Acts 15 shows that Peter had accepted his wrongdoing. There of course remains a need to be discerning in how we go about addressing things (storming into our boss's office and overturning their desk is unlikely to end positively for us) but no one is served by untruth.

And if we're the recipients of such words? In those moments, we have a choice between two paths. We can respond in anger like Ahab, simply ignoring what's been said and dismissing the idea that we could possibly be at fault. Alternatively, we can take some time to reflect and pray, not automatically accepting what's been said, but trusting that their words have come from a place of love, allowing the Holy Spirit to convict us and transform us if appropriate. Receiving and acting on words as Peter did, can take even more courage than it takes to deliver them.

The Prophets

The Old Testament is organised mostly according to genre. The first section (Genesis to Esther) records the history of Israel. The next group (Job – Song of Songs) are wisdom books whilst the remainder are almost all books of prophecy. Ordering the Bible chronologically would cause its own problems. However, an issue with arranging the Bible by genre is that the prophetic messages to Israel (and Judah)[1] are removed from their historical context.

Although prophecy contains predictive elements, the text is primarily addressing the present concerns of the recipients. Therefore knowing when a prophecy was given helps greatly with interpretting the message. On the following pages are brief overviews of each prophetic book, detailing the rough time when the prophecies were given and some of the key themes contained within. Many of the events mentioned are explored in more detail in subsequent readings and therefore it may be helpful to refer back to this section at later points.

Isaiah

Addressed to Judah from the reign of Uzziah to Hezekiah as the Assyrian Empire continued to grow, threatening both Israel and Judah.

- God is more powerful than the Assyrians and would rescue Judah.
- The people need to repent and return to covenant obedience.
- God has a plan which culminates in the arrival of the Messiah, the suffering servant who bears the consequences of the people's sins.

Jeremiah

Addressed to Judah just before and during their time of exile.

- Judah faced punishment due to their continuous spiritual adultery.
- The nation will eventually be brought out of exile and restored.
- A new covenant will be established between God and his people.
- A Davidic king (the Messiah) would be raised up from among them.

[1] Because these books were written after the nation of Israel had been split in two, it can be confusing to keep track of exactly who would have received them. In the following descriptions of each book, the recipients are either the northern kingdom of Israel, the southern kingdom of Judah, the Judean exiles in Babylon or the Judean exiles upon their return.

Ezekiel

Largely addressed to the Judean exiles in Babylon.

- God left their presence due to their sinful and disobedient lifestyles.
- The nation will be restored, and God's spirit placed within us.
- The people need to learn who God is once again.

Daniel

The book of Daniel is formed of two sections. The first six chapters are narrative literature and record several events that he and his friends experienced while in exile in Babylon. The second half of the book consists of apocalyptic visions that Daniel received during this time regarding God's future dealings with Israel and the surrounding nations.

- God hasn't abandoned his people, he's always with us.
- He is Lord over and in control of all the nations of the world.
- That one like a Son of Man will arrive and usher in God's kingdom.

Hosea

Addressed to the nation of Israel towards the end of their independence after living in idolatry for the past hundred and fifty years.

- God isn't like the pagan gods; he demands monotheistic worship.
- Judgement is coming due to the spiritual adultery of the nation.
- However, God's love and mercy meant that deliverance was possible if the people repented from their evil ways.

Joel

Along with Obadiah, Joel is the most difficult prophecy to date. Its traditional position in the Bible implies a time similar to Hosea and Amos, however if this is the case then the absence of references to kings is unusual. Therefore, it could be that the prophecy was given much later, perhaps even at some point between Malachi and the Gospels.

- The people should repent of their sins.
- God desires us to love him wholeheartedly.
- God will pour his Spirit out upon all people.

Amos

Addressed to Israel at the same time as Hosea.

- Very similar to those of Hosea but with an additional focus on the social injustices that were taking place within Israel.
- God would one day restore the people of Israel and give them a permanent home.

Obadiah

Obadiah is an oracle of judgement towards the nation of Edom. There are many times at which such a message would have been appropriate making it one of the hardest books to date accurately. However, perhaps the most likely period would be close to the time of Judah's exile, after Edom had been complicit in the Babylonian destruction of Jerusalem and the killing of inhabitants who had managed to escape.

- God will administer justice on the Kingdom of Edom.
- God will faithfully judge the nations who harm his people.
- God is Lord of the nations.

Jonah

Jonah isn't a prophecy in the same way as the other books listed here are as the book doesn't contain a prophetic word from God to Israel. Instead, it records an event in Jonah's life where he reluctantly delivered a prophecy to the people of Nineveh. Jonah lived during the same time as Hosea and Amos. Therefore, although the exact date of this journey is unclear, it obviously occurred at some point during this period of Israel's history, towards the end of their independence. Although the book doesn't record God speaking directly to Israel, a message which spoke of God's mercy towards those who repent would have likely been of great significance to the people at this point in their history.

- God will be merciful to those who repent.
- God's grace isn't for Jonah, or us, to question.
- God's grace extends even to those we feel have no right to receive it, for that is the definition of grace.

Micah

Addressed to Judah from the reign of Jotham to Hezekiah.

- Assyria would destroy Israel, but Judah would be spared.
- The people need to repent of their sinful and unjust lifestyles.
- God forgives those who repent.
- However, repentance flows from the heart, not sacrifice.

Nahum

Addressed to Judah towards the end of their independence.

- God is slow to anger, however the evil of the Ninevites has not gone unnoticed. Judgement is coming upon them.
- Therefore, Judah need not fear them.
- The Lord is a refuge in times of trouble.

Habakkuk

Addressed to Judah during the same rough period as Nahum. The book reads as a conversation between Habakkuk and God regarding God's actions, or lack thereof, in the face of injustice and sin.

- The injustices of Judah will not go unpunished, God would raise up Babylon to destroy them and then punish the Babylonians for their own evil. God is therefore shown to be Lord over worldly powers.
- God is just and will punish sin.
- Although his ways can be hard to understand, we can still trust him.

Zephaniah

Addressed to Judah during a similar time to Nahum and Habakkuk.

- They should repent of their sins before judgement arrives.
- The evil pagan nations who surround them would too be judged.
- A promise of restoration and a reminder that God still loves them.

Haggai

Written to encourage the returning exiles who are facing opposition to their reconstruction of the temple.

- God (and the construction of his house) need to be a priority.
- God blesses those who put him first.
- This new temple would witness the glory of God in a way the first temple never did.

Zechariah

Written at the same as Haggai with a similar focus of encouragement.

- Our relationship with God is more important than religious rituals.
- The people need to avoid the mistakes of their ancestors, remaining faithful to the covenant and maintaining social justice.
- The Messiah is still coming.
- God remains faithful.

Malachi

Malachi is traditionally thought to be the last prophetic book written. Typically, it's dated to just after the reconstruction of Jerusalem under Ezra and Nehemiah, about 400-450 years before the birth of Jesus.

- God desires a willing worshipper, not obligated worshippers.
- God is worthy of our best.
- The priests have a responsibility to teach and correct the people, and therefore shouldn't ignore or permit sinful actions out of fear of retaliation.
- The Messiah is still coming.
- God is faithful to his promises, however long they take to arrive.

25. Israel is Exiled

2 Kings 15:8-31, 2 Kings 17:1-41

(2 Kings 18:1 – 19:37)

Thus concludes the tragic story of the Northern Kingdom. Israel split from Judah in 931BC and was conquered by the Assyrian Empire in 722BC. Across this period of just over 200 years, Israel had nineteen different kings, yet not one of them was described as having done good in the eyes of the Lord. Every single king did evil and worshipped other gods. However, the worst aspect of their sins was that they encouraged the people of Israel to follow suit. Jeroboam knew that the largest obstacle to him keeping his kingdom was his people's religious ties to Jerusalem. Therefore, immediately following the separation of Israel and Judah, and to discourage them from travelling there, he constructed two golden calves at Bethel and Dan for them to worship instead (1 Kings 12:25-33). From this action stemmed Israel's descent into idolatry (v30).

To be a leader of Christians is a serious responsibility (James 3:1). Leaders wield tremendous influence over those who are entrusted to their care which is why Jesus dealt so severely with the religious authorities of his day (Matt 23). You may not be a church leader yet, but there are a wide range of other activities we can be involved in which impact the faith of others. Youth workers, home group leaders, preachers and worship leaders are just some such roles.

Outside of church, each of us will be a parent, a brother or sister, a friend to a fellow Christian - relationships that are often more significant to their spiritual growth than even the church. Therefore, considering Jesus's words towards those who influence others, it's worth reflecting on the role you play in this process. As a parent, are your actions those that you would wish your children to follow? Are you cultivating an environment where they're able to grow in their faith? (Deut 6:7). As a friend, are you doing your best to help and support them in their walk with God?

It's not the case that we should condemn ourselves if those we know turn away from Jesus. Each person is responsible for their own actions. However, that doesn't excuse us from seeking to live in a way that helps others persevere in faith. Therefore, perhaps ask God to highlight any areas that he wants you to address in order that you may more faithfully lead those who look to you for spiritual wisdom and guidance.

The Kingdom of Israel

King	Bible Ref	Reign[1]	Review
Jeroboam I	1 Kings 12-14	931 - 910	Evil
Nadab	1 Kings 15	910 - 909	Evil
Baasha	1 Kings 16	909 - 886	Evil
Elah	1 Kings 16	886 - 885	Evil
Zimri	1 Kings 16	885	Evil
Omri	1 Kings 16	885 - 874	Evil
Ahab	1 Kings 17	874 – 853	Evil
Ahaziah	1 Kings 22	853 – 852	Evil
Joram	2 Kings 3	852 – 841	Evil
Jehu	2 Kings 9-10	841 – 814	Evil
Jehoahaz	2 Kings 13	814 – 798	Evil
Jehoash	2 Kings 13-14	798 – 782	Evil
Jeroboam II	2 Kings 14	793 – 753	Evil
Zechariah	2 Kings 15	753 – 752	Evil
Shallum	2 Kings 15	752	Evil
Menahem	2 Kings 15	752 – 742	Evil
Pekahiah	2 Kings 15	742 – 740	Evil
Pekah	2 Kings 15	740 – 732	Evil
Hoshea	2 Kings 17	732 – 722	Evil

Spiritual Summary

Over a period of around 200 years, Israel was ruled by 19 different kings. However, despite the warnings from prophets, and repeated petitions that the nation repent of their sins, not one of these kings is recorded as doing good in the eyes of the Lord. Each engaged in idolatrous practices and encouraged the people they ruled to do the same.

Hosea and Amos are the only prophetic books specifically written to Israel. However, Jonah is also recorded as living during this period, and therefore, it's likely that he too was prophesying to the people. His testimony of Nineveh's repentance may have struck a chord with the people, showing God as merciful to all who repent, even their enemies. Elijah and Elisha lived during an earlier part of Israel's history, ministering mostly during and after the reign of Ahab respectively.

[1] Dates are approximate. Overlapping reigns are co-regencies.

Southern Kingdom, includes Jerusalem.

The Kingdom of Judah

King[1]	Bible Ref [2]	Reign[3]	Review
Rehoboam	1 Kings 12-14	931 - 913	Evil
Abijah	1 Kings 15	913 – 911	Evil
Asa	1 Kings 15	911 – 870	Good
Jehoshaphat	1 Kings 22	872 – 848	Good
Jehoram	2 Kings 8	853 – 841	Evil
Ahaziah	2 Kings 8-9	841	Evil
Athaliah[1] Queen	2 Kings 11	841 – 835	Evil
Joash	2 Kings 11-12	835 – 796	Mixed
Amaziah	2 Kings 14	796 – 767	Mixed
Uzziah	2 Kings 15	792 – 740	Mixed
Jotham	2 Kings 15	750 – 732	Good
Ahaz	2 Kings 16	735 – 716	Evil
Hezekiah	2 Kings 18-20	716 – 687	Good
Manasseh	2 Kings 21	697 – 643	Mixed
Amon	2 Kings 21	643 – 641	Evil
Josiah	2 Kings 22-23	641 – 609	Good
Jehoahaz	2 Kings 23	609	Evil
Jehoiakim	2 Kings 23-24	609 – 598	Evil
Jehoiachin	2 Kings 24-25	598 – 597	Evil
Zedekiah	2 Kings 24-25	597 – 586	Evil

Spiritual Summary

Unlike in Israel, the leaders of Judah didn't all turn from the ways of the Lord. The reigns of Hezekiah and Josiah in particular, saw major national projects where altars serving idols were torn down and the temple was restored to its intended function. However, the majority of kings still did evil, helping to cultivate a climate where the worship of pagan gods became increasingly acceptable among the people.

[1] All those listed above were kings except for Athaliah, the only queen who ruled either Israel or Judah.

[2] The kings of Judah are also recorded in 1 and 2 Chronicles.

[3] Dates are approximate. Overlapping reigns are co-regencies.

26. Judah is Exiled and Jerusalem Destroyed

2 Kings 24:1 – 25:12, Jeremiah 2:20-28

(Jeremiah 2:29 – 5:19, Ezekiel 10:4, Ezekiel 10:18-19, Ezekiel 11:5-25)

Although their kings weren't as disobedient as those of Israel, the people of Judah still engaged in the forms of idolatry that had been forbidden by God in his covenant with them (Ex 20:3). Old Testament idolatry can seem very peculiar to us: creating calves out of gold to worship and setting up Asherah poles on the hilltops to list just two examples. However, although the mechanisms of idolatry have changed, the underlying principle of misplaced worship remains.

The phrase "no other gods before me" (Ex 20:3) isn't saying that the worship of idols is only a problem if they're being worshipped ahead of God, it is a blanket prohibition of worshipping any other god in the presence of (before) him. Therefore, we need to be wary not just of worshipping things *above* God but worshipping things *alongside* God. Everything has the potential to become an idol, including many things that aren't inherently bad. There's nothing wrong with wanting to succeed or be loved, but when we start to find our ultimate value in these areas, they have become an idol. We can even turn what we do for God into an idol, craving the recognition and praise that can accompany our ministry.

Idols don't just spontaneously arise in our lives, they grow from something we enjoy or would like, into something that we can't imagine living without, something that we lust after. At their most extreme, idols begin to shape every aspect of our world, including how we interpret scripture and think of God. As this happens, we can find ourselves engaging in and justifying various sins, pursuing them with no regard for others. We can even begin to view people and situations primarily through the lens of their potential to meet our needs.

The impact idols have on our relationships, both with each other and God, mean that we should be proactive in identifying them in our lives. Therefore, it may be worth making a list of things that are of great importance to you and praying through them, asking that God would reveal anything that has already become, or is in danger of becoming, an idol. If anything stands out, pray that God would work to change your heart in that area; that he would give you self-control and a renewed knowledge of his sufficiency in all things.

Why Did the Exile Occur?

The Kingship of David marked the highpoint of Israel's history, as the nation expanded far beyond the original boundaries of the Promised Land, and the Ark of the Covenant was housed in Jerusalem. However, just four centuries later the nation lay in ruin, its citizens taken prisoner across the world. Jerusalem and its temple were destroyed, and the presence of God had left them (Ezek 10:18-19). How did it all end up this way?

Covenant Disobedience (Lev 26:3-38)

Unlike the covenant received by Abraham, God's covenant with Israel wasn't unconditional. Instead, the promised blessings were dependent upon the actions of the people. If they adhered to the covenant they would be blessed (v3-13) and if they didn't, they would be punished (v14-38), spat out from the land God had given them. The rulers of Judah were less consistently disobedient than those of Israel which is why their exile occurred later. However, the covenant violations listed in 2 Kings 17 were true of both nations meaning that, ultimately, both received the punishments they had been warned of.

Weak Leadership

The summary of each king of Israel and Judah tells us whether they did good or evil in the eyes of the Lord. Of the nineteen kings of Israel, not one was classed as doing good and in Judah only eight of twenty rulers were. Their actions, and the example they set, repeatedly encouraged their citizens to disobey the covenant and turn from God.

Lack of Repentance (Isaiah 1:2-20, 1 Kings 17:13-14, 2 Chr 36:15-16)

Having broken the laws of the covenant it would have been perfectly just for God to immediately punish the peoples of Israel and Judah. However, this is not what happened. Prophet after prophet were sent (more than just those whose books are part of the Bible) to warn the people and rulers of God's impending judgement, pleading that they would repent and return to God. However, although there were momentary responses to these messages, the people always fell back into their sinful lifestyles. God's patience is not without limit and therefore, after centuries of violating the covenant, defiling the land and ignoring God's calls to repentance both nations were exiled.

27. Babylon

Daniel 3:1-30, Jeremiah 25:1-14, Jeremiah 29:11-14, Ezra 1:1-4

(Daniel 1:1-21, Ezekiel 34:11-31)

The account of Daniel 3 is one that always stands out to me. Having been exiled to Babylon, the Israelites are faced with the challenge of remaining faithful to God in a foreign land of foreign gods. The King of Babylon demands that they forsake their God and instead bow down in worship to him, yet, even when faced with the prospect of being thrown alive into the blazing furnace, Shadrach, Meshach and Abednego refuse to do so. They know God can save them, *yet even if he doesn't* it makes no difference to their decision. What an incredible attitude to have! Would I have done the same?

In the West we can each face persecution on account of our faith, but I would hope that none of us have been presented with a choice so bleak. Reject God or die! However, this is the present reality for some of our fellow Christians in certain parts of the world, and it's a problem that's growing worse. According to Open Doors (a charity that seeks to serve persecuted Christians) around 310 million Christians experienced high levels of persecution in 2019 while at least 2938 people were killed for their faith. 9488 churches were attacked, a number five times higher than that recorded in 2018.

On the Open Doors website is a list of the 50 places currently deemed the most dangerous to openly identify as a Christian. I would encourage you to find this list and spend some time praying for people you know who are serving in these areas and, more generally, the Christian communities that exist there. That they would be given the strength to remain steadfast in their faith and that they would know the love and peace of God in times of trouble.

We can also pray that their faith would be a witness to those who persecute them. When Nebuchadnezzar looked inside the furnace, he recognized the power of God and allowed the Israelites to again worship their God. Similar testimonies have appeared in recent years of God revealing himself to members of Isis whilst they were enacting their own persecution towards the church. Although we shouldn't desire that the suffering of others continues, God remains able to bring good from any situation, and therefore, in every circumstance, we can pray that God's kingdom is proclaimed.

The Exile

Assyrian Exile

When the northern kingdom of Israel (Samaria) was conquered by the Assyrians, most of the population was dispersed around the Assyrian empire. Foreigners who were brought in to replace them married the remaining locals, meaning that future generations weren't thought to be true Israelites. The tension this brought still existed during the gospels and was a major reason behind Jewish hatred of the Samaritans.

Babylonian Exile

When people talk about "The Exile" they're usually referring to the conquest of Judah by the Babylonian Empire. Over a period of around twenty years the Babylonians gained control of Jerusalem and the surrounding areas, transporting many of the inhabitants to Babylon.

Around 607BC, Jehoiakim became a vassal of Nebuchadnezzar, King of Babylon (2 Kings 24:1). At this time, many of Israel's skilled men were transported to Babylon including Daniel (Daniel 1:1-7). Jehoiakim later revolted and so, in 597BC, Nebuchadnezzar returned, laid siege to Jerusalem and took more people captive (2 Kings 24:10-16) including Jehoiakim's son Jehoiachin. Zedekiah was placed upon the throne, but nine years later he too revolted. Therefore, in 586BC, Nebuchadnezzar returned once more, this time destroying the city of Jerusalem and its temple. Zedekiah was arrested and had his sons killed before him thus ending the line of succession. Although a small group were left behind to work as farmers, most of the population were taken to Babylon as prisoners (2 Kings 25:1-21).

Return

After the Babylonian Empire had been destroyed, King Cyrus of Persia permitted the Israelites to return and rebuild Jerusalem. The return began around 537BC, taking place in four major stages across a period of roughly 100 years. This period is described by Ezra and Nehemiah who record the rebuilding of the temple and walls of Jerusalem. The first group returning were led back by Sheshbazzar, the newly appointed governor of Judah, shortly after the decree of Cyrus (Ezra 1). The next group arrived with Zerubbabel a short amount of time later (Ezra 2) and the third with Ezra in 458BC (Ezra 7-8). The final group were led by Nehemiah and returned in 445BC (Nehemiah 2).

28. The Temple is Rebuilt

Ezra 3:8 – 4:5, Ezra 4:24 – 5:2, Haggai 1:1 – 2:9, Ezra 6:14-22

(Ezra 4:6-23, Ezra 5:3 – 6:13)

Behold, I am the Lord, the God of all flesh; is anything too difficult for Me? (Jer 32:27).

The Books of Ezra and Nehemiah record the efforts of the returning exiles to rebuild the temple (Ezra) and walls (Nehemiah) of Jerusalem. Once the Assyrians had conquered the Northern Kingdom of Israel (Samaria), most of the population were dispersed around the Assyrian empire and replaced with foreigners. Because of this, the people of Samaria were no longer considered 'proper Israelites' leading to the tensions recorded in Ezra. The Samaritans opposed construction of the temple (Ezra 4:1-5 & 24) and the walls (Ezra 4:6-23) for nearly one hundred years. However, despite the many challenges that they faced, God's prophets encouraged the people to persevere and, through the power of God, both projects were completed.

As we walk with God, we will each encounter obstacles that seem insurmountable. The appropriate response though, isn't to lose hope, but to come before God in prayer as repeatedly demonstrated in Nehemiah. Prayer is the thread that holds the book together and so, in all sorts of situations, Nehemiah's response to problems isn't to try and solve them in his own strength, but to hand everything over to God. When responding to a question from the king we hear that before answering, Nehemiah quickly prayed (Neh 2:4). Just a simple "Lord help me" is enough, God knows our needs. Through prayer, Nehemiah rebuilt the walls in just 52 days!

Having been living in exile, there were likely many Israelites unsure about how God would now treat them. However, throughout this period of opposition, the Israelites witnessed the same faithful God who had cared and provided for their ancestors. Despite the exile, and the destruction of the temple, he remained a God they could trust, and who would come through for them in their hour of need. In every situation that we face, we can be encouraged by the faithfulness of God and the message from Jeremiah above: that whatever we're facing, and however bleak our prospects look, the God we worship is more than capable of coming through for us.

The Second Temple

Overview

The second temple of Jerusalem was built by the returning exiles from Babylon under the leadership of Zerubbabel. Despite significant opposition (Ezra 4-6) construction was finished in 516BC, around twenty years after they arrived. It was built where Solomon's Temple had stood and was designed in a similar way, maintaining the layout of the original tabernacle: a courtyard, the holy place and the most holy place. In 20BC, work was undertaken by Herod to markedly increase the size of the temple complex. This project lasted until 64AD, just six years before it was destroyed by the Romans (p133).

Inferior to The Original

'Who is left among you who saw this temple in its former glory? And how do you see it now? Does it not seem to you like nothing in comparison?' (Haggai 2:3)

wonder why no Shekinah

These words are spoken as the temple is nearing completion. Due to the length of the exile, there were still a few people who had seen the original temple and were disheartened by what they now saw. Although both temples were similarly sized, the original was far more elaborately decorated and, of greater importance, more impressive spiritually. Both the Ark of the Covenant and the Shekinah[1] glory of the Lord had been present within, and there's no indication that either were ever seen in the rebuilt temple.

Promises of Glory and Peace

'The latter glory of this house will be greater than the former,' says the Lord of hosts, 'and in this place I will give peace,' (Haggai 2:9)

Despite the people's discouragement, the final lines of this prophecy are full of hope for what will later be accomplished here. Although God wasn't present as a visible Shekinah cloud, he appeared in a far more significant way in the person of Jesus who, around five-hundred years after Haggai had spoken, walked through this building. His death brought forgiveness to the world and it's in this temple that the veil separating us from God was finally torn in two, reconciling us to him.

[1] A rabbinic term for the dwelling of divine presence on earth.

Bridging the Testaments

From the end of Malachi until the start of the gospel narratives roughly 400 years passes that the Bible provides very little information about. The residents of first century Israel knew their national history and therefore the gospel writers had no need to restate it (another example of how the Bible was written for us but not to us). However, this silence poses a challenge for us today because the social and religious situation in Israel changes drastically over this time. The world of Jesus is a very different place from the world of the Old Testament.

The Old Testament narrative ends with the exiles having returned to Jerusalem and rebuilt the temple. For the next two centuries the nation was ruled by a series of High Priests who answered to Persia, until the Greeks, led by Alexander the Great, conquered the Persian Empire and much of the Middle East (332BC). Greek culture spread throughout the Mediterranean, greatly aiding the future New Testament evangelists who were able to preach in Greek and be understood wherever they went. This is also why the New Testament was written in Greek.

Upon his death, Alexander's empire was divided between his four generals, two of whom are important to events in Palestine: Ptolemy governor of Egypt and Seleucus governor of Syria. Palestine was located between them and was therefore regularly fought over with Jerusalem changing hands on many occasions. Eventually, the Seleucids took firmer control of the area and began dismantling the religious customs of the Jews. The king Antiochus (203BC), removed the Jewish High Priest and sold the position to the highest bidder. In 171BC, hearing reports that the king had died, the Jews revolted. However, the report was incorrect and upon his return Antiochus responded with fury. He slaughtered 40,000 people and defiled the temple by having pagan priests kill a pig upon the altar (an unclean animal in the eyes of the people) and spreading its blood throughout the entire sanctuary.

Around seven years later, the Jews, led by Judas Maccabaeus, revolted once more and this time managed to overthrow their foreign rulers. This event and the ensuing restoration of the temple are remembered each year during the Festival of Hanukkah. Independence was maintained for around a hundred years under the leadership of the Hasmonean dynasty until, in 63BC, Hyrcanus was challenged for the throne by his brother Aristobulus. Both sought help from the nearby Roman armies who, upon reaching Jerusalem, were allowed into the city by supporters of Hyrcanus. However, after capturing the temple, the Romans decided to keep control of the city for themselves. Although the Jews maintained a degree of autonomy, their power was severely restricted. They were obliged to pay tribute to Rome and the kingdom which the Hasmoneans had grown was split up. Antipater was appointed as Procurator of Judea and subsequently crowned his sons as kings of Galilee and Judea. The Judean king was Herod the Great (Matt 2:1-2).

Accompanying the centuries of political turmoil in Israel were major religious changes. Hellenization (the spreading of Greek culture) was perceived as a threat to the Jewish religion, and so during this time two key religious groups emerged: the Sadducees and Pharisees. Sadducees were typically born into the aristocracy and willingly embraced Greek culture. They argued that only the Torah (Genesis – Deuteronomy) was the authoritative word of God and so observed strict purity regulations. However, they lacked a belief in the supernatural and therefore denied the idea of resurrection (Matt 22:22-33). They attributed everything to free will and therefore viewed their successes as their own.

The Pharisees arose in opposition to Greek culture, strongly believing that their religion should be free from liberal Greek influences. They considered not just the Torah but later oral traditions, including the rest of the Old Testament, as authoritative. Consideration was given as to how the law should be applied to contemporary issues, however, as Jesus pointed out, they were often blind to the heart of the original laws. The Pharisees strongly opposed the Sadducee view of spirituality and resurrection (Acts 23:6-9) and so sought to balance the sovereignty of God with human free will. They were exceedingly popular amongst the masses and considered themselves to be the shepherds of God's people, teaching them how they should act in accordance with God's law.

Jesus is born into this new world, therefore even a basic knowledge of these religious and political tensions will help us to better understand some of the key issues in his ministry. For example, why Jesus spent so much of his time interacting with the Pharisees, why the Sadducees asked certain questions, and why Pilate was so keen to appease the angry crowds and avoid another rebellion. Another key point to understand is that the people's vision of a Messiah was of someone who would come and rescue Israel from her foreign oppressors as he had done many times before, both during the Old Testament and in the period we have just reviewed. Much of Jesus's ministry involved interacting with people who struggled to comprehend a Messiah who showed no interest in defeating the Romans and granting them independence.

29. Jesus is Born

Luke 2:1-21, Matthew 2:1-12, Luke 15:11-32

(Luke 1:1-80, Luke 2:22-40, Matthew 1:1-17)

Much of the Christmas story runs contrary to expectation. Jesus's birth to the unmarried Mary was a social disgrace, a humiliation for her husband and could well be the reason that there wasn't room for them in Joseph's hometown of Bethlehem. He wasn't born into a priestly or royal family, but to a carpenter from Nazareth. How could anything good come out of Nazareth? (John 1:46).

This pattern of the unexpected continues with the first groups of people to meet Jesus. The shepherds were at the bottom of society's ladder, uneducated and unimportant. The Magi were foreigners (Gentiles) engaging in astrology and magic, both sinful practices in the eyes of the Jews. It was to these people, not the religious leaders, that Jesus first appeared, because it was for these people that he came into the world. Jesus's heart is for the ignored, the persecuted, the sinner that's 'beyond the reach of God' – because the truth is that no one's beyond his reach. This is the heart of the parable of the prodigal son, that however far we are from God, he will still run out to embrace us upon our return and, by placing a robe upon our shoulders, welcome and adopt us as his children. There's no one too sinful to be forgiven, no one too lost to be found, no one who's unimportant in the eyes of God.

As well as being a source of personal encouragement, these words should be the lens through which we see those around us. A defining feature of Jesus's ministry were his clashes with people who objected to those he spent time with, represented in this parable by the older son. They had no compassion for the sinner, only condemnation. We must be wary of letting similar attitudes develop in our lives; remembering the love Jesus showed to all people, even those who hated him (Luke 23:34, Rom 5:6-8). This doesn't mean that we refuse to stand up for what's right or ignore the moral teachings of scripture. However, it's easy to develop a mindset where we see certain people as being so far from God that we begin to treat them differently, forgetting that ultimately it's Jesus who causes people to change from a life of sin. We can choose to act like the Pharisees, outraged that Jesus would associate with such people (Mark 2:16) or we can seek to walk in the same way as Jesus by showing them love and compassion. It's the love of God that transforms people and it's a love without limits.

Prophecies Fulfilled

Then beginning with Moses and with all the prophets, He explained to them the things concerning Himself in all the Scriptures. (Luke 24:27).

All of the Jewish scriptures (our Old Testament) find their fulfilment in Jesus. A key demonstration of this is how Jesus relates to the numerous prophecies written concerning the Messiah. Over 300 of them can be identified, describing his birth, ministry and death, a selection of which are listed in the table below.

Prophecy	O.T. Ref	Fulfilment
Descended from David	2 Samuel 7:12-16	Luke 3:31
And Judah	Genesis 49:10	Luke 3:33
And Abraham	Genesis 12:3	Luke 3:34
And Adam	Genesis 3:15	Luke 3:38
Born in Bethlehem	Micah 5:2	Luke 2:4
To A Virgin	Isaiah 7:14	Luke 1:34
Proclaimed by Another	Isaiah 40:3-5	Mark 1:1-11
Ministered in Galilee	Isaiah 9:1-2	Mark 1:14
Performing Miracles	Isaiah 35:5-6	Mark 1:34
Among the Gentiles	Isaiah 42:1-4	Mark 5:19-20
Would be Rejected	Psalm 118:22	Mark 6:1-6
And Betrayed for 30 pcs of Silver	Zechariah 11:12-13	Matt 26:15
Considered a Sinner	Isaiah 53:12	Matt 26:57-68
Sentenced to Death	Isaiah 53:8	Matt 27:26
Would be Mocked	Psalm 22:7-8	Matt 27:29
And Spat Upon	Isaiah 50:6	Matt 27:30
Have His Skin Pierced	Psalm 22:14-16	John 19:34
And Clothes Divided	Psalm 22:18	Matt 27:35
Laid in a Rich Man's Tomb	Isaiah 53:9	Matt 27:57-61
Would Rise from the Dead	Psalm 16:8-11	Matt 28:1-10
As he had Promised	Matthew 16:21	Matt 28:1-10

30. The Ministry of Jesus

Mark 2:1-28, Mark 4:1-20

(Mark 4:21 – 5:43)   Mark 4:21 end   Mark 5:1-20
                                                    21-43

The parable of the sower is one of the most famous parables Jesus spoke. Like most of what Jesus says it's presenting something quite complex (how people respond to God) and explaining it in terms that made sense to the people who followed him. However, whenever Jesus speaks, there tends to be a great amount of depth we can overlook. Consider the different seeds. As a Christian I can read this parable and rightly conclude that I'm like the seed that landed in good soil. I've heard the gospel message and decided to follow Jesus and so I can tick this parable off as one I don't need to worry about anymore. But is everything that straight forward? Is there nothing else that I can learn from it?

As well as representing how people respond to the gospel message, the imagery found in the parable can also be used to describe how people respond to God's voice in general. The readings today show Jesus interacting with various people. In each instance he explained what he was doing but for many of the people present his words had no effect. They fell on rocky ground.

This can sadly be true of us too. What was the sermon you heard last week about? What did you take away from it? What has changed as a result? If you can answer these questions then great, but too often we listen to someone talk without hearing what they are saying. We may feel a sense of conviction in the moment, but it's quickly forgotten and replaced with more pressing concerns such as what we'll be doing for the rest of the day or which biscuit we'll select at the end of the service! God's word is landing on the path, not growing in our lives.

Therefore, in order that his word bears fruit in our lives, we need to be intentional about cultivating good soil in our hearts. Through prayer the Holy Spirit will help us, but we can also take simple practical steps. For example, in order to better remember what has been said, it may help to make notes during a sermon or to listen to a recording a few days later. Specifics will look different for each person but behind it all is an attitude of wanting to hear from God. Spend some time praying through this area and considering how you can better prepare the soil of your heart to joyfully receive his word.

Israel at the Time of Jesus

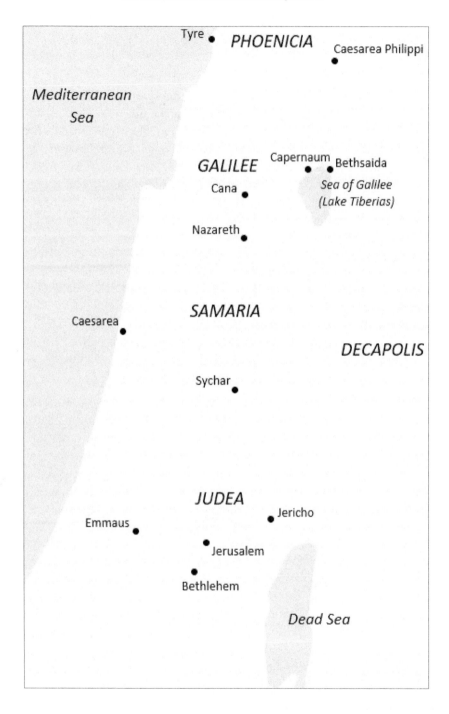

I Am Sayings of Jesus

The seven "I am" sayings of Jesus are a unique feature of John's Gospel. Each reveals something specific about the person and ministry of Jesus, whilst also deliberately evoking the words God used to identify himself to Israel, "I am who I am" (Ex 3:14).

I am the Bread of Life (John 6:48)

Context: During Jesus's sermon following the feeding of the 5000.

Bread was the staple food of an Israelite's diet. In the temple there were always twelve loaves of bread signifying the provision of God towards Israel (twelve loaves for twelve tribes) by reminding them of how God had fed their ancestors with manna during the Exodus. The image of eating his body as bread which occurs later in this chapter foreshadows the last supper and the saving work of his death. With this title, Jesus is claiming to be our great provider, sustaining us not just physically but also spiritually, delivering us from the powers of sin and death.

I am the Light of the World (John 8:12)

7 days in length at beginning of harvest.

Context: Shortly after the Feast of Tabernacles (p45).

As already discussed, this feast was a reminder of the journey that their ancestors had made from Egypt to the Promised Land. During the festivities a great candelabra was illuminated which, like the lampstands of the tabernacle and temples, represented God's presence as a pillar of flame that had guided their ancestors through the wilderness (Exodus 13:21-22). Just as God guided them, so too Jesus guides us through life, always with us whatever we're going through, wherever we are.

The light in the wilderness was the very presence of God and therefore whilst each "I am" statement carries with it the implication that Jesus is professing to be God, this is one of the clearest examples of him publicly making that claim. The rest of the chapter illustrates this point and ends with the people attempting to kill him for blasphemy. Jesus is the light shining in the darkness, revealing God to the world (John 1:4-5). Called to be lights of the world, we are charged to do the same, revealing God to those around us through our words and deeds. Bringing light where there is darkness, hope where there is despair, forgiveness where there is none and life where there is death.

I am the Gate ... I am the Good Shepherd (John 10:7, 10:11)

Context: During a discourse with the Pharisees.

The Pharisees were the self-appointed shepherds of God's people. Well respected by the people, they took it upon themselves to keep the people in adherence to God's law and distinct from Roman and Greek culture. However, their many exchanges with Jesus highlight the fact that they'd done a terrible job of this, imposing unnecessary burdens on people and often failing to keep the same standards they expected of others. Worse than this, the gospels also show them working to steer people away from Jesus who they had failed to recognise was their long-awaited Messiah.

By way of comparison Jesus declares himself to be the Good Shepherd, protecting his flock (believers) from evil. We have the assurance that once we give our lives to Jesus, he will not lose us, and we shall enjoy eternity with him. This is emphasised more fully through the gate (door) title which refers to a role performed by shepherds. During the summer the sheep would be kept outside in stone pens which were entered through a small opening. Overnight the shepherd would sleep in this gap, preventing the sheep from wandering into danger and protecting them from external threats. The only way into the pen was through the shepherd, just as Jesus is the only way to the Father (John 14:6).

I am the Resurrection and the Life (John 11:25)

Context: After Lazarus has died and Martha seeks the help of Jesus.

Although denied by the Sadducees, the Old Testament promises a day where the dead shall be raised back to life (Isaiah 26:19, Daniel 12:2). In this passage Jesus makes the claim that it's through him that these words will be fulfilled and proceeds to demonstrate this authority by bringing Lazarus back from the dead.

Although Lazarus wasn't the first person who Jesus brought back to life, it's important to remember that the ministry of Jesus took place over several years across the nation. Therefore, he wasn't surrounded by the same people each time. Those who witnessed this miracle may have seen nothing else of Jesus. As believers we have a hope that even though we will all die, we will likewise all live. Upon death we will each join him in paradise before being raised to new life as part of God's new creation.

I am the Way, the Truth and the Life (John 14:6)

Context: Comforting his followers in the build up to his death.

It's clear through various exchanges that the disciples had the same sorts of preconceived ideas as their fellow Israelites about what the Messiah would do. They, therefore, found it hard to understand some of the statements Jesus made, particularly those concerning his approaching death. Even as he was arrested shortly after this exchange, one of them sought to free Jesus by attacking his accusers (Luke 22:50).

Jesus knew his disciples faced a future of persecution and opposition. He therefore implores them to remain fixed on the truth of who he is and the claims he's been making about himself, emphasising once again that he is indeed God. Throughout history, philosophies and religions have emerged offering new perspectives on existence and the world, claiming to speak the truth. However, as Christians we know that the truth people seek can only be found in Jesus. Through him we see the world for what it truly is: a creation crying out for restoration (Rom 8:19-22); and hear the truth of who we are: sinners in need of God's grace (Rom 3:23) but also beloved children of God (Rom 8:14-16). The only way, the only path to eternal life is through believing in Jesus.

I am the True Vine (John 15:1)

Context: Again, whilst with his followers in the build up to his death.

In the Old Testament (Isaiah 5:1-7, Psalm 80:7-19), and the teachings of Jesus (Matt 21:33-46), the imagery of a vine or vineyard is often used to refer to Israel. This title can therefore be viewed as Jesus claiming to be the fulfilment of Israel and the role that God gave her as his nation: to draw the surrounding peoples to him through their example. This isn't removing Israel's position as God's chosen people. Rather, it's a declaration that Jesus is accomplishing what Israel was unable to do.

Attention is then turned to the disciples. Knowing that he won't be with them much longer, Jesus provides encouragement by explaining that as he sends them into the world, they will still be able to depend on him. More than this though, they're warned that this will be essential if their actions are to produce the same fruit as Jesus's own ministry. This truth should be the cornerstone of our own service to God, reminding us that it's impossible to accomplish his work in just our own strength. Through abiding in him all things are possible, and we can be assured that our lives with him will be exceedingly fruitful.

31. Jesus the Son of God

Mark 8:27 – 9:13, John 14:1-11

(John 1:1-34, John 8:12-59)

We live in an age where professing to know the truth can be interpreted as an arrogant, perhaps offensive claim – something that can be observed in the attitude people often have towards religion and Jesus. How can you claim to have sole possession of the truth? How can Christianity be the only way to God? These are fair questions. However, the reason we believe those things isn't due to arrogance, but because Jesus *makes those very claims*, declaring that he's "the way, and the truth and the life; no-one comes to the father except through" him (John 14:6).

Some people think Jesus was just a good moral teacher or, in line with Islamic teaching, that he was merely a prophet. However, the problem with these perspectives is that Jesus doesn't allow us to accept them. The actions of Jesus repeatedly demonstrated that he saw himself as God and as a result the authorities had him killed. To make such a claim was blasphemous and thus, according to their laws, deserved death … unless the claim was true. In his ministry, Jesus continually invited people to consider who he was, a question that remains as relevant today as it was to those in first-century Israel. Either he was crazy or lying and therefore not worth worrying about, or he really is the son of God and we should pay close attention to what he said.

As Christians, we of course believe the latter, which is why it's so important to share the gospel with those around us. This doesn't mean that we go out of our way to confront and upset others, we must be wise and discerning with regards to how we address different situations. Instead, it's about having an attitude where we're in no way ashamed of the claims Jesus makes, recognising how important it is for people to accept who Jesus was and what he said.

The recent TV series about the Chernobyl nuclear disaster explores the consequences of ignoring the truth. Due to costs and political pressure the authorities continually ignored the inherent flaws of their nuclear reactors. Eventually disaster came because although we may find it uncomfortable, the truth cannot simply be washed away. Pretending that Jesus didn't claim to be God and that he didn't claim to be the only way to eternal life, doesn't make those claims untrue. And of course, being true, they're the most important truths in history.

Claims of Deity

A question sometimes levelled at Christians is why we consider Jesus to be God when he never makes that assertion himself. It's true that when we read the gospels, it can appear as though Jesus is silent on the issue. However, this observation is caused by us coming to the gospels wanting Jesus to reveal his deity in a way we would expect, standing up and shouting in plain language "I am God!". What becomes clear though, as we view Jesus through the lens of a first century Israelite, is that through what he did and said Jesus was doing just this.

During his ministry Jesus regularly engaged in actions synonymous with God. Forgiveness of sins was something only God could do, yet Jesus openly pronounced that people's sins had been forgiven (Mark 2:5). Similarly, the Sabbath was a day set aside by the command of God. When Jesus claimed to be Lord of the Sabbath (Matt 12:8) there is only one way to interpret what he was saying because God himself is Lord of the Sabbath. Each of the seven "I am" statements in John carry with them the idea of deity, particularly the claim that Jesus is the Light of the World (John 8), just as the light of God had guided the Israelites through the wilderness as a pillar of fire. The claim resulted in fury from the Pharisees with the resulting argument culminating in the clearest public claim Jesus made to be God, "before Abraham was born, I Am". When Moses was concerned that his fellow Israelites would not believe God had sent him, he was told to say that I Am sent you (Ex 3:14). Jesus's use of this title is therefore an explicit declaration that he is God.

The crowd's furious reaction to this statement highlights another point often missed when people look for evidence that Jesus claimed to be God, the reactions of those around him. The Pharisees and religious leaders regularly accused him of blasphemy (Luke 22:66-71), even when it isn't immediately clear to us why that was the case. To assume someone is God isn't a normal thing to do, even if that person is performing great miracles. Israel's history was full of prophets and people who, empowered by God, did amazing things – however none of them were ever thought of as being God. On the other hand, with Jesus, both his enemies and followers recognised the claims he was making, even if they came to different conclusions. When his followers proclaimed him as Lord, Jesus didn't correct but rather commended them (John 13:13). Although Jesus often asked people not to share what they had seen, he never once discouraged people from their worship of him as God.

32. The Arrest of Jesus

Jeremiah 31:31-34, Mark 14:12-42

(Hebrews 2:5-18, Hebrews 4:14-16, Hebrews 7:1 – 8:13)

In the Jewish Priesthood, one man was appointed as the High Priest. He served as a mediator between the people and God and, on the Day of Atonement, performed the rituals which atoned for the sins of the people. It was the only time of the year that the High Priest could enter the Holy of Holies and stand in God's presence. In the New Covenant that Jesus establishes, it is he who is designated as our High Priest forever in the presence of God, enabling us to approach him without fear. However, to mediate on behalf of the people, the High Priest needs to understand what the people are experiencing. In order to become our High Priest, Jesus needed to come to earth as a human (Heb 2:14-18).

Because of the many miracles that he performs, it can be easy for us to focus on Jesus's deity whilst overlooking his humanity. However, awaiting arrest in the Garden of Gethsemane, we can clearly see this side of him. Three times Jesus asks whether there's any other way (Matt 26:39-46), three times the answer is no. He becomes grieved to the point of death, so distressed that he begins to sweat blood (Luke 22:44).

Over the course of his life Jesus experienced a great amount of suffering. He was rejected by the people he came to save (John 6:60-66), his friends (Luke 22:54-62), and even his family (Mark 3:21). He was mocked and insulted (Matt 27:39-44), betrayed by one of his closest followers for just thirty pieces of silver (Matt 26:14-16). He was tempted in the same way as us (Luke 4:1-13) and was angered by the same forms of injustice that we can, likewise, grow frustrated with (Mark 11:15-19). He knew what it was like to experience pain, and not just the physical pain associated with his death. During his life he would have had friends die and his absence from the gospel narrative makes it highly likely that his father Joseph had died before Jesus began his ministry.

As we pray to God about the issues we're facing, we can be encouraged that we aren't praying to someone who has no idea what we're experiencing. Instead, we're praying to a Father who, whilst still fully God, has suffered in the same ways that we do, and who can therefore empathise with our sufferings.

The New Covenant

Over the course of the Bible, God makes two communal covenants with his people. The Old Covenant is centred around observing the Law of God and involved making various offerings in accordance with God's instructions. Due to the sins of the people these religious ceremonies needed to be repeated day after day, year after year.

During the Passover meal before his arrest, Jesus announces that he's establishing a New Covenant. Through his death on the cross there's no longer a need for continual offerings. Instead, Jesus offered himself upon the cross as a perfect sacrifice, bringing an end to the practices of the Old Covenant. This New Covenant transforms how the former operated as outlined in more detail below.

A New People & Timeframe (Jer 32:40)

The Old Covenant was a temporary covenant with the nation of Israel that was to be used until God replaced it with something greater. That occurs with the inauguration of The New Covenant through the death and resurrection of Jesus. The New Covenant is an everlasting covenant for everyone who believes in Jesus, whether Israelite (such as the first believers) or Gentile.

A New High Priest (Heb 4:14 – 5:10)

As mentioned previously, Jesus is appointed as a new and greater High Priest, one who never needs to be replaced upon death and one who's, therefore, forever seated at the right hand of the Father. The shedding of his own blood accomplished for all time what the Day of Atonement did on an annual basis.

A New Way of Approach (Heb 4:16, 10:1-18)

The Old Covenant and associated system of offerings provided a means for the worshipper to approach God through the death of animals and the ascension of whatever was burnt upon the altar. Purity regulations and the distribution of blood were also necessary to maintain the sacred space of the temple. Under the New Covenant these rituals are no longer required. Our representative is forever in the presence of God and through him we have constant access to the father.

Filled with the Spirit (Ezekiel 36:26)

Central to the functionality of the New Covenant, is the indwelling power of the Holy Spirit. Under the Old Covenant, the Spirit of God was given to specific individuals at specific times. However, at Pentecost the Spirit was poured out upon all flesh in fulfilment of the prophecy found in Joel 2:28-29. As Christians we no longer need to go the temple in order to meet with God because he now lives within each of us.

A New Way of Transmitting the Law (Jer 31:31-34)

When Israel received the Old Covenant, the nation (and specifically the priesthood) were tasked with ensuring that each generation understood the character and requirements of God. The New Covenant ushers in a time where the laws of God are written on the hearts of believers. The Holy Spirit convicts us of our sins and transforms our hearts and minds to better represent Jesus in our lives.

The Same Path to Salvation

The focus on laws in the Old Testament can lead us to believe that Jesus (and the New Covenant) is changing the mechanism of salvation[1] from works to faith in God. However, it was never the case that people were "saved" by strictly following rules - a point Paul repeatedly emphasised in his writing (Romans 1-4, Galatians 1-3, Ephesians 2:1-10). Diligently following the law will never see someone declared righteous (in right standing with God) because it's an impossible task. In the Old Testament people were saved through their faith in God, nothing more (Hab 2:4, Gen 15:6, Rom 4). The same is true today. We're saved not by following a set of rules but through recognising our inability to save ourselves and instead relying on the work of Jesus.

[1] Whilst acknowledging that salvation is a term that describes far more than just going to heaven when we die, the discussion here is concerned with that more limited definition which tends to be what people have in mind when considering the faith / works argument.

33. The Death of Jesus

Mark 14:43 – 15:47, Romans 5:1-21

(Isaiah 52:13 – 53:12, Hebrews 9:1 – 10:25)

You call Me Teacher and Lord; and you are right, for so I am. If I then, the Lord and the Teacher, washed your feet, you also ought to wash one another's feet. For I gave you an example that you also should do as I did to you. (John 13:13-15).

Is there a bigger challenge in the Bible than this? To love others as Jesus loves me. There's nowhere I feel more convicted on this subject than the account of his arrest, trial and execution. He's first betrayed by one of his closest followers for thirty pieces of silver before the rest of his followers abandon him. Peter, the rock Jesus intended to build his church upon, denied even knowing him. Finally, he's accused of blasphemy by the religious authorities. The appropriate penalty for such a crime was death, however the twist of the gospels is that it's not Jesus who was guilty of blasphemy, but his accusers. In his death upon the cross Jesus bore the penalty they deserved, and in doing so freed them from the wrath of God. Jesus suffered all this because of the love he had for those same people, a love that encompasses all mankind.

Our actions towards others flow from how we perceive them. Therefore, if we desire to imitate the actions of Jesus, then we should first focus upon cultivating a Christ-like mindset, something that can be assisted by using his actions as a lens through which to see those around us. For if Jesus thought that they were worth dying for, then how can I possibly justify treating them any differently? How could I stand before Jesus and convince him that I was right, and he was wrong? However much someone irritates us, or causes us problems, they remain as loved by God as we are. He's just as interested in a relationship with them as he is a relationship with us.

When we start viewing people in this way, our actions and attitudes will inevitably change. It's not something that necessarily happens overnight, particularly towards those who have deeply hurt us. But over time, through prayer and the power of the Holy Spirit, we will find ourselves ever better mirroring the love of Jesus. The wonder of following Jesus is that despite our constant failings, God's love for us is constantly unfailing. May we each be committed to showing this same love to those we encounter.

Christ as Fulfilment

The ministry of Jesus fulfils the prophecies made about him, as well as the religious rituals that were a shadow of what was to come. Some of this has already been considered with respect to Jesus's role as our new and greater High Priest whilst below are short sections exploring a few additional ways in which Jesus fulfils the Levitical system of offerings.

Passover

Jesus is our new and better Passover lamb. Free from any blemish he was put to death to save us from death, his blood covering us from the penalty that our sin warrants. Through his death we are brought out from our slavery to sin and into the promised land of fellowship with him. In communion we remember Jesus as our saviour in the same way as the Israelites remembered their deliverance from Egypt during the Passover meal.

Scapegoat

Jesus is our new and better scape goat. Year after year the scapegoat had the sins of the community placed upon it before being driven out from the community and killed. Bearing the sins of the world, Jesus was likewise taken out of Jerusalem and killed upon the cross. Through his death our sins are removed in a way that needs no repetition. We are free from condemnation and welcomed as children of God.

Offering

Jesus is our new and better offering. As the animals were put to death on behalf of the worshipper, Jesus is likewise slain on our behalf upon the cross. However, death was merely the beginning of the offering process and, therefore, just as the animal was burnt in the fire of the Lord and ascended to the heavens in order to represent the worshipper before God, the same is true of Jesus. Rising from death he ascended to heaven and is seated at the right hand of the Father for all eternity. Through this final offering the veil in the temple was torn in two and the separation between us and God, which sacrifice ministered within, was removed. Jesus forever intercedes to the Father on our behalf and through him we're able to boldly approach the throne of God, a throne once hidden from view but now available to all through Jesus.

34. The Resurrection

John 20:1 – 21:25, Psalm 32:1-11

(1 Corinthians 15:1-58, Luke 15:11-32 [1])

The Psalms speak to us in a way that's quite unique in scripture. They deal with real issues from a first-person perspective as David, or another of the authors, contemplate the challenges that they're facing. In Psalm 32, David addresses that feeling of guilt that each of us can experience. There are different types and intensities of guilt depending upon what's been done and the ramifications of our actions, but guilt will always be an obstacle to relationship, including our relationship with God.

When reflecting upon how he denied Jesus, I think it would have been impossible for Peter not to feel a great sense of guilt. He had abandoned a close friend, leaving him to suffer an unjust death of extraordinary pain. Yet when Jesus is with him on the beach, he doesn't challenge Peter over what he's done, but simply asks "do you love me?" Peter's love for Jesus, and clear remorse at what he had done (Luke 22:62), meant that all his failings were forgiven.

We live in a culture where there's a cost associated to everything, and as such it can be difficult for us to comprehend the forgiveness of God. However, in dying upon the cross, Jesus paid that cost and so just like David and Peter, we can be assured that when we confess our sins to God, they are completely forgiven. Once the lost son had returned to his father, he was given a pair of shoes. When Jesus was telling this story, if you owed someone money, then you would either pay them back or, if that was impossible, pay off your debts through working for them. Servants were often employed for this reason and were distinguished from other residents by walking around barefoot. In providing his son with shoes, the father was making it clear to him, and those around, that there was nothing to pay back. His 'sins' had been forgiven.

It makes no sense. He had just cost his father half of his estate and yet doesn't owe a single penny? His brother is outraged at this injustice. However, forgiveness in this instance depends solely upon the grace of the father and therefore it didn't matter what anyone else, including the returning son, thought. Even if you find it hard to understand how God could forgive someone like you, be assured that he has (1 John 1:9).

[1] This reading was also used on page 97.

The Resurrection of Jesus (1 Corinthians 15)

The bodily resurrection of Jesus is the central claim of Christianity. It's the pillar that our entire faith is built upon and therefore without it, everything falls apart. If Jesus simply died upon the cross, then he was merely a man crucified by the Romans. Just one of thousands to have met a similar fate. We may think it wise to follow his teaching, but it's not imperative that we do so and he certainly isn't someone we should be keen to surrender our lives to. As Paul outlines in his most significant teaching on the subject (1 Cor 15), without the resurrection we're still dead in our sins with no hope (v12-19). We have no assurance of life after death (v20-28) or the future victory of Christ at his return (v50-58). If Jesus was never raised back to life, we should be "most pitied" among men (v19).

However, if the resurrection did occur, everything changes. During his life, Jesus stated several times that he would die and then be raised back to life (Mark 8:31, 9:31, 10:33-34). Therefore, in being raised from the dead, Jesus's claims about himself are revealed to be true (Acts 17:31). He's the son of God; the Messiah who is forever worthy of our worship. Although several people in the Bible were brought back to life, Jesus's resurrection was something quite different. Those people later died and therefore, in a sense, their coming back to life was more akin to a resuscitation. Jesus though, was raised back to life in a body that will never perish. He is a new and final Adam (v45), the firstfruits of those who have died (v20). He is the resurrection and the life and therefore we can be confident that through faith in him we too will live, even though we die (John 11:25). Therefore, although we may grieve for fellow believers who pass away, we need not despair as those without hope (1 Thess 4:13-18) because we know that they are with Jesus in paradise and will be raised to new life with him upon his return. We have a hope that can never be taken from us; a hope that we can hold onto through trial and suffering (Heb 6:18-20, 2 Cor 4:16-18).

Two thousand years after Paul wrote to the Corinthian church, the idea that Jesus rose from the dead remains a major stumbling block and a common source of questions for people exploring Christianity. For this reason (and those outlined above regarding its importance to our own faith) it's a topic that we should seek to understand. Something that we can be confident took place and be able to answer basic questions about, because although people who are crucified tend not to come back to life, there's compelling historical and logical evidence that Jesus was indeed raised from the dead.

Evidence for the Resurrection

Some of the facts about the resurrection are fairly uncontroversial:

1. *Jesus was a citizen of Israel who was crucified by the Romans around 30AD.*

2. *In the first century after Jesus was crucified, there were a group of people utterly convinced that he had been raised from the dead.*

3. *This belief spread rapidly across the Mediterranean as the Christians managed to persuade thousands of others that the resurrection had occurred.*

4. *The Jewish authorities were opposed to this message and, through persecution, sought to prevent it from spreading. Therefore, if the authorities could have proved Jesus was still dead, they would have.*

5. *Consequently, we can also conclude that the tomb Jesus was placed in was empty.*

It's difficult to dispute these facts. They are attested to not just by the Bible but by various other historical sources from this time and basic common sense. Of course, just because people were claiming that they had encountered the resurrected Jesus doesn't automatically mean that they did. Instead, there are three broad explanations that make sense:

1. *They believed they had seen him but were mistaken.*

2. *They were lying.*

3. *They actually did encounter Jesus.*

To be genuinely mistaken the claimants must have experienced a form of dream or hallucination. However, simply dreaming Jesus had risen from the dead doesn't change the fact that he had died. The tomb would still have contained his body, which, as has already been considered, we can be confident it did not. Secondly, hallucinations don't happen en masse. Paul states that Jesus appeared to over 500 people at the same time, most of whom are still alive (v6), thus challenging those with doubts to go and question them. Finally, the gospels record the disciples physically interacting with Jesus (John 20:24-29) not just seeing him.

If the disciples were lying it's hard to understand their motives for doing so. Paul placed himself "in danger every hour" by claiming that Jesus had risen from the dead (v30-32). The apostles faced great persecution and, with the likely exception of John, were all killed for their faith. If they were lying, then surely facing death (often an incredible painful form of death) they would have confessed to making everything up. The fact that none of them did this should give us great confidence in their claims. People don't die for something they know to be a lie.

It also makes no sense that each gospel mentions a woman as being the first person to encounter the resurrected Jesus. In first-century Israel, the word of a woman was worthless in a court of law. They were untrusted witnesses and, therefore, to claim that they saw this miracle opened the Christians up to ridicule and distrust. The only reason for doing so was to accurately record what had taken place.

If we discount the possibilities that the disciples were deceived or lying, then all we are left with is the option that they were telling the truth. I am yet to hear anything that better explains the early growth of the church and the actions of the disciples that makes more sense than the genuine, bodily resurrection of Jesus.

35. The Great Commission

Matthew 28:16-20, Acts 1:1-11, Matthew 25:14-30

(Ezekiel 3:17-19, Romans 1:16-17, Romans 10:9-17)

Among the final words that Jesus spoke to his disciples is what has become known inside the church as the Great Commission. The charge that as Jesus discipled them, they're now to disciple others. It's a task that's as applicable to us two-thousand years later as it was to them. Something that will forever be the mission of the church.

Discipleship refers to the means by which we become more Christ-like and the ways in which we support others to do the same. It's a process that continues throughout the life of a believer and therefore it's slightly unfortunate that Jesus's instructions here are often solely associated with telling unbelievers about Jesus. That first step is of course the most important, but discipleship encompasses so much more than just this initial point of conversion.

Each of us are called to play a role in the discipleship of others, whether that be through ministering to those who don't yet believe or teaching and supporting those who already do. In fact, for most of us, it will be a combination of the two as we daily encounter people at various stages of their journey with God, including those who haven't yet begun theirs. In the parable above, the master gave his servants talents of money that represent the gifts God has bestowed upon each of us. Therefore, just as the master expected his servants to use their gifts for his purposes, we're called to use the gifts that God has given to us in service to him. We can either live in obedience to this instruction, or be like the servant who buried what was given to him and simply waited for his master to return.

There are various reasons that can stand in the way of us more actively serving God. We may feel scared, unsure how to teach others about Jesus, or believe we're incapable of doing so. Perhaps we simply have no interest in seeing others grow in their faith. Over the next few pages, we'll look at what the Bible reveals to us about these sorts of objections. However, something that cannot be denied is Jesus's desire that we tell others about him. That we are a church seeking to develop disciples and spread the kingdom of God throughout our communities.

The Growing Church

*But you will receive power when the Holy Spirit has come upon you;
and you shall be My witnesses both in Jerusalem, and in all Judea and
Samaria, and even to the remotest part of the earth. (Acts 1:8).*

These words from Jesus to his disciples form the introduction to Acts, a
book which proceeds to record how these words were fulfilled.

Acts 1-7: Jerusalem

*The word of God kept on spreading; and the number of the disciples
continued to increase greatly in Jerusalem (Acts 6:7).*

The first seven chapters are focused on events within Jerusalem such as
the arrival of the Holy Spirit, the establishment of the church, and the
opposition that the first Christians faced from the Jewish authorities.

Acts 8-12: Judea and Samaria

*So the church throughout all Judea and Galilee and Samaria enjoyed
peace, being built up; and going on in the fear of the Lord and in the
comfort of the Holy Spirit, it continued to increase. (Acts 9:31).*

The message then moved beyond the largely Jewish Jerusalem and to
the Gentiles. There are some major differences between these cultures
and, consequently, various theological questions arise. For example, do
the Gentile Christians need to be circumcised or adhere to the food
laws of the Torah? These issues are addressed for the first time at the
council of Jerusalem (Acts 15) and remain key themes of later epistles.

Acts 13-28: To the Farthest Parts of the Earth

*This became known to all, both Jews and Greeks, who lived in Ephesus;
and fear fell upon them all and the name of the Lord Jesus was being
magnified. ... So the word of the Lord was growing mightily and
prevailing. (Acts 19:17,20)*

The remainder of Acts looks at how the church spread into the wider
world through the missionary work of Paul, Silas, Barnabas and other
evangelists. The book concludes with the message reaching the centre
of first century civilization, Rome.

The Holy Spirit

The Holy Spirit is a member of the trinitarian God we worship: Father, Son & Holy Spirit. Although a major focus of the New Testament, his presence can be observed throughout the Bible. In the Old Testament he is referred to as the Spirit of The Lord and is described as falling upon individuals to help them at specific times (Exodus 31:2-5, 1 Samuel 10:10, 1 Samuel 16:12-13). The leaders of Israel were dependent upon the Spirit in their ministry just as we are today.

However, in the New Testament, our means of encountering the Holy Spirit changed greatly. Jesus's death and resurrection tore the veil which separated us from God and consequently, from Pentecost, the Holy Spirit now dwells within each believer (1 Cor 3:16) performing many roles in our lives and the wider world. Subsequent reflections will consider the general help he provides in our ministry whilst below are outlined some of the additional roles that he undertakes in us.

Convicting the World

But I tell you the truth, it is to your advantage that I go away; for if I do not go away, the Helper will not come to you; but if I go, I will send Him to you. And He, when He comes, will convict the world concerning sin and righteousness and judgment; concerning sin, because they do not believe in Me; and concerning righteousness, because I go to the Father and you no longer see Me; and concerning judgment, because the ruler of this world has been judged. (John 16:7-11)

Repentance, turning from a life of sin, is a key component of choosing to follow Jesus. However, before repentance is possible, people first need to acknowledge the sin that's present in their lives; to recognise that they are living contrary to God's ideals. This change in perspective is called conviction and is something brought about through the work of the Holy Spirit.

When we share the good news of Jesus with others, we can attempt to persuade them with complex arguments or accounts of God's work in our lives. However, ultimately, it's the Holy Spirit who convicts them of their need for God and draws them into relationship with him. Conviction continues beyond this point as well. As believers, the Holy Spirit brings an increased awareness of our own failings and dependence on the grace and love of God.

Growing Fruit in Our Lives (Sanctification)

Now the deeds of the flesh are evident, which are: immorality, impurity, sensuality, idolatry, sorcery, enmities, strife, jealousy, outbursts of anger, disputes, dissensions, factions, envying, drunkenness, carousing, and things like these, of which I forewarn you, just as I have forewarned you, that those who practice such things will not inherit the kingdom of God. But the fruit of the Spirit is love, joy, peace, patience, kindness, goodness, faithfulness, gentleness, self-control; against such things there is no law. Now those who belong to Christ Jesus have crucified the flesh with its passions and desires. If we live by the Spirit, let us also walk by the Spirit. (Gal 5:19-25).

As Christians we're instructed to live in a way that imitates the life of Christ (1 John 2:6). To call this a challenge is quite an understatement! No person ever becomes a Christian from a place of perfection and no Christian, however hard we try, will ever be able to fully replicate Christ in our own lives.

However, if we allow him to, the Holy Spirit works to make us more Christ-like in our thoughts and actions. This process is known as sanctification and is evidenced through our lives producing ever more of the fruits listed above. We will never achieve perfection but there are many testimonies of people that were engaged in all sorts of damaging, sinful activities being radically transformed by the Holy Spirit.

Interceding for Us

In the same way the Spirit also helps our weakness; for we do not know how to pray as we should, but the Spirit Himself intercedes for us with groanings too deep for words; and He who searches the hearts knows what the mind of the Spirit is, because He intercedes for the saints according to the will of God. (Romans 8:26-27).

In this chapter, Paul describes how as believers we live in anticipation of our future resurrection – filled with the Holy Spirit but still inhabiting a fleshly body. We await being united with Christ at the resurrection, but we're not there yet. An aspect of this arrangement is that we don't always ask for what we should or according to God's will. Sometimes we don't even know what we should pray for. Fortunately, God knows us better than we know ourselves and therefore the Spirit, aware of exactly what we need, is continually at work interceding for us.

Bestowing Gifts

Now there are varieties of gifts, but the same Spirit. And there are varieties of ministries, and the same Lord. There are varieties of effects, but the same God who works all things in all persons. But to each one is given the manifestation of the Spirit for the common good. For to one is given the word of wisdom through the Spirit, and to another the word of knowledge according to the same Spirit; to another faith by the same Spirit, and to another gifts of healing by the one Spirit, and to another the effecting of miracles, and to another prophecy, and to another the distinguishing of spirits, to another various kinds of tongues, and to another the interpretation of tongues. But one and the same Spirit works all these things, distributing to each one individually just as He wills. (1 Cor 12:4-11).

As with many themes in the Bible, the idea of gifts or giftedness can be quite complex. Therefore, before looking at the gifts of the Holy Spirit, it's worth clarifying that we're all gifted in various non-miraculous ways. By this, I mean that we each have certain interests, skills, personalities, etc, that allow us to minister in ways that others cannot. Someone with an ability to play the clarinet at a professional level is going to be far better placed to evangelise within an orchestra than someone who isn't even able to identify a clarinet. Even things such as our age can open doors that may not be available to others, something that's particularly the case for the youth and children in our churches. Having each been created by God, we can still consider these things as being gifts from him which is why they are discussed elsewhere in Paul's writings on the topic (Rom 12:3-8, Eph 4:1-16).

The gifts listed above are known as the gifts of the Holy Spirit and are uniquely found in Christians. They are bestowed by the Spirit as he deems fit, not based on anything we've done, but on the needs of the wider church. Therefore, although there's nothing wrong with desiring gifts, we shouldn't think better or worse about ourselves based on how present they are in our lives. We're all uniquely equipped to serve him.

Certain people experience these gifts regularly and are thus considered gifted. However, this doesn't mean that the gifts are only available to such people. The Holy Spirit is within each follower of Jesus, and therefore, as he's the source of these gifts, every believer is capable of prophesying or seeing healing when they pray for people. In my own life there have been occasions when I have been given supernatural knowledge about a situation. However, as this doesn't occur regularly, I wouldn't claim to have the gift of prophecy.

Teaching

Yet we do speak wisdom among those who are mature; a wisdom, however, not of this age nor of the rulers of this age, who are passing away; but we speak God's wisdom in a mystery, the hidden wisdom which God predestined before the ages to our glory; the wisdom which none of the rulers of this age has understood; for if they had understood it they would not have crucified the Lord of glory; But just as it is written, "Things which eye has not seen and ear has not heard, and which have not entered the heart of man, all that God has prepared for those who love Him." For to us God revealed them through the Spirit; for the Spirit searches all things, even the depths of God. For who among men knows the thoughts of a man except the spirit of the man which is in him? Even so the thoughts of God no one knows except the Spirit of God. Now we have received, not the spirit of the world, but the Spirit who is from God, so that we may know the things freely given to us by God, which things we also speak, not in words taught by human wisdom, but in those taught by the Spirit, combining spiritual thoughts with spiritual words. (1 Cor 2:6-13).

The Holy Spirit is the Spirit of truth (John 16:13-14) who teaches us in all things. Firstly, he reveals truths about God and our faith. As we read scripture, he can illuminate teaching that we had never seen before that perhaps we need for the season of life we find ourselves in. He brings understanding concerning what passages reveal about God and how we can apply their lessons to our own lives. Through his working we're able to better comprehend the nature and workings of God.

The Spirit also informs how we perceive the world and its need for God. He gives us discernment to recognise what lies beneath worldly events and attitudes, therefore enabling us to discern spiritual things and distinguish the way of the world from the way of God, the way of truth. We are better able to understand the motivations of people and how they fit into what the Bible teaches us about human desires and our longing to be reconciled to God.

Finally, he provides us with practical teaching for our lives by speaking wisdom into situations that we or those around us are facing. We are shown how to best serve those who are suffering in their time of need and taught how to respond to conflict in a productive way. His voice guides us through life, helping us to make decisions that are in line with God's will. He is our helper in all things, at all times.

36. Pentecost

Joel 2:28-29, Acts 2:1-47, 1 Corinthians 3:5-7

(Acts 3:1 – 4:31, Luke 15:11-32 [1])

In the parable of the lost son, one of the three gifts bestowed to the son upon his return was a signet ring, something used in the ancient world to seal letters and sign documents. If a letter arrived bearing the mark of such a ring, then the recipient knew from where it had come. Therefore, when the son received this gift, he was being entrusted with the power to act on behalf of his father.

For Christians, the ring in this story symbolises the Holy Spirit – a gift which is likewise bestowed upon us when we return to God. The Spirit has many roles in the life of a believer, but in terms of mission, it's the tool by which all things are accomplished. Once Jesus had been raised from the dead, I'm sure the disciples were desperate to go and proclaim to everyone what they had just witnessed. However, when Jesus speaks to them for the final time, this isn't what he commands. Instead, he instructs them to wait for the Holy Spirit to arrive. Only then will they be capable of accomplishing what God has called them to do.

The Book of Acts records how the church grew from a small group of people in a room in Jerusalem, to a family of believers spread throughout the Mediterranean. Many individuals and miracles are recorded, but at the heart of everything is the work of the Holy Spirit. When Peter spoke on Pentecost it was the Holy Spirit that convicted the hearts of the crowd and led to 3000 people being saved. As Peter and John walked towards the temple it was the Holy Spirit that brought healing to the lame beggar who approached them (Acts 3:6) and when they testified before the Sanhedrin it was the Holy Spirit that showed Peter what to say (Acts 4:8). Paul's words to the Corinthians reinforce this point. He is merely a servant. It's God who is worthy of praise for what has happened since Paul first spoke to them.

God has called the church to be his witnesses throughout the world but what should be incredibly freeing for each of us, is knowing that behind the words we speak is the power of the Holy Spirit. That wherever we are, whatever we are doing, the Holy Spirit is beside us accomplishing more than we could ever do by ourselves. The same power that raised Jesus from the grave lives in us!

[1] This reading was also used on page 97.

Pentecost

Pentecost took place during the Jewish Festival of Weeks (p44) and was a clear fulfilment of Joel 2:28 where God promised to pour out his Spirit on all people. The offerings presented to God during this festival involved giving the first fruits of the wheat harvest in anticipation of God's provision throughout the harvest. In a similar way, the people who gave their lives to Jesus at Pentecost were the first fruits of his new harvest: a harvest that will continue until he returns once more and brings this age to a close.

There are also a series of parallels between the events recorded at Mt Sinai, where God first met with Israel, and those which occurred on Pentecost where God first met with the church. Some of these are listed in the table below:

Mt Sinai (Ex 19 – 40)	Pentecost (Acts 2:1-41)
God appears with fire and wind.	God appears with fire and wind.
The presence of God falls upon the mountain.	The presence of God falls upon the disciples.
God establishes his covenant with Israel.	Although inaugurated upon the death of Jesus, Pentecost is when the church received the fullness of the New Covenant.
Israel receives the gift of The Law.	The church receives the gift of the Holy Spirit.
The law of God is written on stone tablets.	The law of God is written on the heart of the believer.
God comes to dwell among his people within the tabernacle.	God comes to dwell among his people within each believer.
3000 die due to the power of the law.	3000 are given new life due to the power of the spirit.

The Trinity

Belief in the trinity is one of the fundamental doctrines that distinguishes genuine Christianity from religions such as Mormonism and Jehovah's Witnesses. Although the term itself isn't found in the Bible, it has been used by the church to describe the three-person God that scripture clearly does teach. Although there are certain details of the trinity that we can understand, it's a concept unlike anything we have on earth and will therefore always be beyond our ability to fully comprehend.

One God – Three Persons

The most fundamental principle of the trinity is that our one God is formed of three persons: Father, Son (Jesus and often thought to be the angel of the Lord in the Old Testament) and Holy Spirit (or Spirit of the Lord). Each person is distinct, with their own roles, but are equally God. A popular summary is that the Father is the head of God, the Son reveals God and the Spirit performs the work of God.

Brings Clarity to Scripture

The Bible repeatedly testifies that God is one (Deut 6:4, 1 Tim 2:5) yet at the same time seems to contradict this statement. God creates mankind not in "his" but in "our image" (Gen 1:26). Jesus claims to be the God of Abraham (John 8) but prays to God (Luke 22:42) and when confronting the sins of Ananias and Sapphira, Peter equates lying to the Holy Spirit with lying to God (Acts 5:3-4). The epistles also regularly talk of the combined work of Father, Son and Holy Spirit (1 Peter 1:2, 2 Thess 2:13) and, in his final instructions, Jesus tells his disciples to baptize people in the name of the Father, Son and Spirit (Matt 28:19). It's these sorts of passages that gave rise to trinitarian theology.

A Model for Relationship

The trinity is a model of perfect community and so there are various aspects of the trinity that can inform the different relationships we have (marriages, friendships, those within structures of authority, etc). For example, the place for roles within relationships (and that those roles do not devalue anyone as what any member achieves has been achieved as a collective), and what biblical submission looks like. At the heart of everything though, is sacrificial love towards one another. A love that brings forth unity and that we're too called to exhibit (Phil 2:1-8).

37. The Conversion of Saul (Paul)

Acts 9:1-31

(Acts 6:1 – 8:3)

In recent years there has been a vast increase in the number of superhero films being released. Seemingly every month, a new tale arrives of an individual blessed with incredible powers and abilities overcoming their enemies. The Bible is similarly filled with accounts of such 'heroes' winning impossible battles and performing great miracles. However, something that regularly strikes me when reading these passages, is how ordinary these people are. We're not presented with flawless individuals. Instead, the passages expose, and occasionally focus upon, their many weaknesses.

We're told about Peter, who denied knowing Jesus out of fear for what would happen to himself. Jonah, who hated the Ninevites so much he refused to tell them about God, lest they repent and be forgiven. David, who impregnated another man's wife and, in order to cover up his actions, had the man killed in battle. Perhaps worst of all was Paul, who despite professing to serve God, had dedicated himself to persecuting the few Jews who had *actually recognised* their Messiah when he arrived. Yet despite his past, Paul would go on to proclaim Jesus to thousands of unbelievers and would now be considered the most influential church teacher outside of Jesus.

God has chosen to act in this world through his followers. It should therefore be a great comfort that the historical figures who led his people were flawed individuals like us. It's easy to think poorly of ourselves and believe the lie that we're unable to serve God; that we're not good enough or smart enough. However, the Bible shows us time and again that this isn't the case. It's filled with accounts of ordinary people with all their imperfections, performing extraordinary things through the Holy Spirit who empowers them.

We should rejoice in knowing that we're not alone in our service to God, but that he's the one building his Kingdom through us. The Peter that boldly stood up during Pentecost and preached to the crowds of Jerusalem, was unrecognisable from the Peter who had denied Jesus just several weeks earlier. Whatever reason you have to not serve God, he is far stronger than your weaknesses.

The Life of Paul (Saul)

Early Life

Paul was born Saul in the city of Tarsus around 5AD. He was skilled in tent-making (Acts 18:1-3) which was therefore likely a family trade, but as a child went to Jerusalem to be taught by the well-respected Pharisee Gamaliel. This education would have exposed him to a range of religious and philosophical traditions, making him well suited for the missionary work that he spent the second half of his life engaged in.

Pharisee

Saul considered himself a Pharisee (Acts 23:6) and a strict follower of the law (Acts 22:3). His first mention in the Bible occurs when a crowd, listening to the words of Stephen, throw their clothes before him (Acts 7). This act indicated what was about to happen and therefore, by failing to intervene, Saul granted them permission to carry out their sentence and stone Stephen to death. Despite his former teacher warning against trying to stop the Christian movement (Acts 5:34-39), Saul remained convinced that they were mistaken. He became an influential figure in the persecution of the early church until his encounter with Jesus on the road to Damascus (Acts 9:1-22, 22:4-9).

Ministry

During his ministry as an apostle, Paul went on four recorded missionary trips throughout the Mediterranean, planting churches across the region including in several major urban centres such as Corinth and Ephesus. He also wrote many letters to churches and fellow believers: teaching, rebuking, encouraging, and advising them. Thirteen of these letters are found in the New Testament.

The final chapters of Acts record Paul being questioned by the Roman authorities in Palestine, an event that enabled him to appeal that he be taken to Rome and have his case heard by Caesar. Upon arriving he was kept under house arrest for two years before, according to tradition, being released. However, once the Romans began their persecution of Christians, Paul was imprisoned once more and this time sentenced to death. As a Roman Citizen he was entitled to a more dignified execution than crucifixion and was therefore beheaded.

The Journeys of Paul

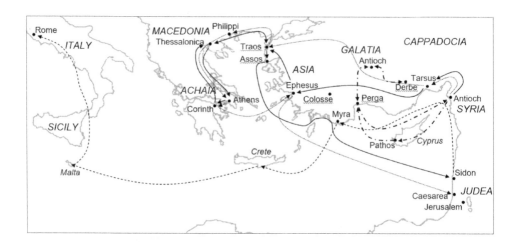

1ˢᵗ Trip (Acts 13-14) ▪ ▪ ▪ ▪ ▪ ▪ ▶

Having left Antioch, Paul travelled through Cyprus before continuing into the east of modern-day Turkey and planting several churches. He returned via a very similar route.

2ⁿᵈ Trip (Acts 15:36 – 18:22) ⋯⋯⋯⋯⋯▶

After revisiting some churches from his first trip, Paul journeyed on to Corinth through Galatia, Philippi and Thessalonica. He returned to Antioch via Ephesus and Jerusalem.

3ʳᵈ Trip (Acts 18:23 – 21:14) ───────▶

His third missionary trip saw Paul visit many of the same areas that he had travelled to previously. He finished this journey in Jerusalem.

4ᵗʰ Trip (Acts 27:1 – 28:30) ▪ ▪ ▪ ▪ ▪ ▪ ▶

Having been arrested in Jerusalem, Paul made use of the opportunity afforded to him and asked that his case be heard by Caesar. His journey to Rome took him via Crete and Malta and is recorded in the final two chapters of Acts.

38. To the Ends of the Earth

Acts 15:36 – 16:40, 1 Timothy 1:12-17, 2 Corinthians 5:10-21

(Acts 17:1 – 18:22)

The ministry of Paul took him on four recorded journeys throughout the Mediterranean. He was guided by the spirit (Acts 16:6-8), not by his own desires, exhibiting a model we should all seek to follow. The people in our communities are no less valuable to God than those in the impoverished parts of the world that people tend to associate with Christian mission. However, wherever God wants us to be, we should all strive to have the same passion for telling others about Jesus that Paul demonstrated in his own life.

Paul's ministry is centred on the grace of God (Rom 1:16-17), and how could it not have been, in light of how God had rescued him from the path to ruin he had been heading down. This first-hand experience of the grace and mercy of God propelled him to share the gospel with everyone! Immediately after his conversion and healing, Paul began preaching in Damascus, which led the people to try to kill him, and after escaping to Jerusalem he preached there too before again having to escape before he was killed! (Acts 9:17-30).

We can sometimes view our faith as a private matter that shouldn't be discussed in public. That everyone has the right to their own beliefs. However, when we fully appreciate what God has done for us, and what he therefore offers to everyone, how can we possibly stay silent? This is the heart of mission. Giving our time and attention to those without God, because of the abundance that God has blessed us with. This doesn't necessarily have to involve proclaiming the gospel in the town centre every day. Sometimes just mentioning in conversation how God has recently helped us can prompt people to examine their own lives and approach us about Jesus from a place of genuine receptiveness. But when the opportunity arises, we shouldn't hesitate to joyfully share with them what it means to follow Jesus.

Jesus gave his life for us so that we could enter into a relationship with him. As a result, we've been adopted as his children and are indwelt by the Holy Spirit. He's always with us, guiding, teaching and comforting us as we walk through life and rather than fearing the inevitability of death, we can look forward to eternity with him. How can these truths not compel us, as they did Paul, to share Jesus with those we love?

Themes of The Epistles

Most of the New Testament is made up of epistles, letters written to either churches or pastoral letters to individuals. They were written by various apostles (including Paul who wrote over half) across a period of around fifty years with most dated to between 50 and 65AD. Although the letters address specific issues being faced by the recipient, the shared Mediterranean culture means that several themes regularly appear, some of which are outlined below.

Distinguishing Christianity from Judaism

The first converts to Christianity were almost exclusively Jewish. In their eyes, Jesus was the Messiah and therefore the Old Covenant had now been replaced with a newer and better covenant that was accessible to Gentiles. The significance of these changes cannot be overstated. The first Christians possessed a radically altered worldview and were thus completely distinct from their Jewish brothers and sisters.

The challenge for the first believers was determining what these changes meant to their different traditions and customs. For example, Jews had for hundreds of years circumcised each new-born to represent their entry into the community of God. Certain believers felt that Gentile converts needed to be marked in such a way too. Another topic discussed in Romans and 1 Corinthians concerns the dietary regulations of the Old Testament. Historically, Jews were forbidden from eating different foods and so there were those who believed that this should also be required of new believers.

The middle chapters of Acts and many of Paul's writings seek to bring clarity to these conversations. On the topic of circumcision, it was decided that Gentile converts did not need to perform this ritual, with greater emphasis placed instead on entering God's community through the process of baptism. Regarding food, although each person was encouraged to act in accordance with their own conscience, the apostles were clear that God had declared all foods to be clean.

Jews placed a great significance on their history, ancestors and traditions. These elements defined them as a people and thus distinguished them from the Gentiles who lived among them. However, Paul encouraged his audience to stop labelling people as either Jew or Gentile. They were all united in Christ and should therefore treat one another as equals.

The Grace of God

The grace of God, as demonstrated to us in the free offer of eternal life available to all who believe in Jesus, was just as counter-cultural then as it is today. How can it be that God loves me enough to die in my place? How can it be that I don't need to do something to earn this love?

Paul spends time wrestling with these sorts of theological questions as well as practical questions many believers have when hearing about God's grace. Does the fact that Jesus has forgiven me now mean that I can do whatever I want and still get to heaven? How can I be considered free from sin when I still regularly make mistakes? The most extensive exploration of this topic is found in the first eight chapters of Romans where Paul explains our predisposition to sin, our need for Jesus and the effects of his death and resurrection on both us and the wider world.

Handling Persecution

During the time that the Epistles were written, the church experienced a great amount of persecution. New Christians were confronted with not just intellectual obstacles to belief but the very real chance of death, and therefore the apostle's writings towards them regularly included encouragement to persevere. Believers were reminded of their hope in Jesus (1 Pet 1:3-5) and his presence beside them in all that they face.

However, an aspect of this subject that we don't always recognise is that the apostles saw persecution as something to rejoice in. This didn't mean they went out of their way to get thrown into prison and killed. Rather, it was an appreciation that to suffer for their faith meant that they were experiencing what Jesus had promised would fall upon those his followers and was therefore a sign that his spirit was resting on them (1 Pet 4:12-14).

Church Practices

The Jewish religion was organised around the temple and priesthood. In Jesus, those systems were made spiritually obsolete, and therefore a new structure was established in the form of the church. New rituals such as baptism and the Eucharist were introduced, and a new hierarchy of authority and accountability was established. The Epistles, specifically 1 Corinthians, 1 Timothy and Titus outline these practices, respond to common questions and provide pastoral wisdom to those in positions of leadership within the early church.

The Christian Life

Throughout the early church, believers faced the challenge of living according to principles that were radically different from their local culture. For example, the worship of idols surrounded believers in Corinth to such a degree that it was challenging to even purchase food that hadn't previously been offered to another god. An additional key difference involved the promotion and acceptance of sexual practices that were far removed from what God desires of his followers.

Many of the letters contain practical advice for how Christians should conduct themselves in different spheres of life. Some passages address specific cultural issues such as the value placed on earthly wisdom in Corinth or the prevalence of Gnosticism in Colossae. However, found throughout the Epistles are principles of love, peace, forgiveness, and abstaining from sins such as envy, drunkenness, and sexual immorality (among others) - attitudes that we remain called to live by.

False Teachers

Another issue which the early church faced was the ministry of false teachers. Many churches in the Mediterranean were established by the apostles and evangelists, but those people were only capable of being in one place at a time. The theology they taught was different to anything people had heard before and therefore as well as having many questions, believers were also susceptible to the words of false teachers. Anyone could claim apostolic authority and the reality of the spiritual realm means that miracles alone aren't evidence that someone follows God.

The letters of Peter and John tackle this problem at length, encouraging those they have taught to remain faithful to the faith they were baptised into. The pillars of Christianity, later expressed in the creeds we recite at church, are undebatable among genuine Christianity. Therefore, the people could be confident that someone preaching an unresurrected Christ or a non-trinitarian God were to be avoided.

In the ancient world a lack of communication meant false teachers were often able to cause significant harm before correction could be brought. Today we have the opposite problem. The internet allows anyone to post Christian teaching, but much of what is available contains all sorts of unhelpful or false information. As with the early church, we should always weigh what we read with scripture.

Gnosticism

Gnosticism is a broad term including many different beliefs around at
the time the Epistles were written. Because of this doctrinal variety, the
specific issues being addressed by the apostles will differ from letter to
letter, however there are some basic similarities which form the basis of
gnostic teaching.

Firstly, Gnostics believed that everything spiritual was good and that
everything physical was evil. A consequence of such a binary belief was
a difficulty in accepting that Jesus was a physical being. How could the
creator of the universe inhabit a corruptible, weak, ultimately evil body?
In fact, if his body were evil, how could he have been without sin upon
the cross? An additional ramification was that their actions on earth were
considered insignificant because they were carried out whilst having an
evil physical form. It was seen as impossible for physical humans to do
anything good.

Another belief was that there was a higher level of knowledge that could
only be obtained spiritually. This knowledge was the path to salvation,
not the work of Jesus. Clearly this teaching was completely contrary to
the words of scripture but, in a culture where Gnosticism was prevalent,
it was a common source of disputes. Colossians and 1 John in particular,
deal with some of these common problems that a gnostic perspective
could have upon church doctrine and the faith of believers.

39. Paul's Final Letter

2 Timothy 1:1 – 4:22

The Book of 2 Timothy is likely the last book that Paul wrote. He'd faced death many times over his life, but it's clear that whilst writing this book, he knew his time on earth was drawing to a close. I wonder how he felt at that moment, looking back at all God had accomplished through him. Over four recorded journeys, Paul was instrumental in the planting of many churches across the Mediterranean and would therefore have played a role in leading thousands of individuals to Jesus. However, despite all that he was involved in, I'm sure there were still moments of regret from his ministry. As a human leader it's certain that he made mistakes and as an evangelist I imagine he pained for those he hadn't been able to reach. He had desired to spread the gospel to Spain (Romans 15:24-28), but there's no biblical record of him ever doing so.

Our journey through life will be much the same. There will be moments of celebration and times we wish had gone differently. That person who we never got around to telling about Jesus or that conversation that went so terribly. We can regret decisions that we made, relationships that were lost, hurt we caused. It's, of course, good to reflect on the mistakes we make. How else do we learn? However, amid regret, we can easily lose sight of the things God has accomplished through our lives. The people we discipled, either as leader or friend, who are still walking with God. Events we were involved in that saw people give their lives to Jesus. Situations where we were able to share the love of God with those who so desperately needed it.

It's a conscious decision to move from a place of regret to one of praise, celebrating God for what he's done, but it's a decision we should all seek to make. Regret can lead to discouragement or feelings of inadequacy and consequently impact both our ministry and relationship with God. In his letter to the Thessalonians, Paul encourages them to continually thank God (1 Thess 5:18), and although we tend to think of this solely in terms of the earthly blessings we receive, it's just as important to thank God for the work he's done in us and through us (1 Thess 1:2-3). When we intentionally remind ourselves of such things, it becomes easier to look beyond the negatives and instead focus on the many ways in which we have faithfully and fruitfully served God. Perhaps spend some time today remembering these things and rejoicing in God's work.

Persecution of The Church

A major theme of the New Testament is the persecution of Christians,
fulfilling the words Jesus had spoken about what awaited his followers
(Luke 21:10-24, John 15:18 - 16:33).

Jewish

Christians suffered persecution from the very beginning. Acts 5
describes the apostles being beaten for their beliefs whilst Acts 7 records
the stoning of Stephen under the approving eye of Paul who, when
converted, was on a mission to round up Christians in Damascus.
Despite the church initially consisting of Jewish converts, the Christians
were considered heretics for claiming that the Messiah had come. The
idea that Jesus was the Messiah, also led to the obvious conclusion that
the religious authorities (and people of Israel) had killed their Messiah -
an implication they didn't happily accept. The Jewish persecutions
recorded in the Bible were largely the result of these tensions.

Roman

In 64AD the Great Fire of Rome occurred and destroyed large parts of
the city. Although it's widely thought that Nero instigated the fires to
allow for the construction of his new palace, the blame was instead
placed upon the already unpopular Christians. Irrespective of who or
what ultimately caused the fire, it signalled the beginning of a nearly
200-year period of Roman persecution which, within several years, had
resulted in the execution of both Paul and Peter. According to tradition
Paul, being a Roman citizen, was beheaded whilst Peter was crucified
upside-down at his request as he felt unworthy to die in the same way
as Jesus.

Temple Destroyed

In 66AD the Jews rose up and revolted against their Roman rulers. At
around the central point of what turned out to be a seven-year conflict,
just before Passover in 70AD, the Roman army laid siege to Jerusalem.
They surrounded the city to prevent supplies from reaching the rebels
and in August of the same year breached the inner walls. The temple
was completely destroyed and thousands were massacred. The religious
practices of Israel, made obsolete through the death and resurrection of
Jesus, ended and have not recommenced since.

40. Hope

Revelation 21:1 – 22:21

(Revelation 1:1-20, Revelation 4:1-11)

Faith, hope and love. The great virtues of our faith, regularly appearing together in the letters to the New Testament church (1 Cor 13:13, Col 1:4-5, 1 Thess 1:3,). They're distinct, yet each essential to the Christian life. If we lack faith, then we can have no confidence in the words and promises of Jesus. If we lack love, then we'll fail in our command to reflect Jesus to those around us. If we lack hope, then we have no reason to endure when we inevitably encounter pain and suffering.

As Christians we live in light of the crucifixion and resurrection of Jesus (events that demonstrated his conquering of death and the powers of evil) but before the victories he has won are made complete. We will all, in some way, experience the pain of sickness and death; endure times of suffering. One of the defining features of the early church was the persecution they encountered - something that sadly continues today in many parts of the world (p91). It's therefore unsurprising that the apostles frequently address this topic in their writings, reminding their audience of the hope that they have in Jesus (Heb 12:1-3, 1 Pe 1:3).

When we consider the hope we have, we tend to focus on our ultimate hope - spending eternity with Jesus as described in Revelation. A time when creation is finally restored to the vision of Genesis 2 and we again dwell in the presence of God. A time when all forms of suffering finally cease, and those who are in Christ are raised into new imperishable bodies to reign with him forever. We have the hope that death is not the end, that this life is just the beginning. And therefore, although we may grieve, we need not despair.

Our hopes, though, are more than just these distant hopes. As we have walked through the Bible, we've encountered a God who should instil all manner of hopes in us, whatever we're facing. In sickness we can hope in a healing, miracle working God. In times of scarcity we can hope in a God of provision. When we feel lost or alone, we can hope in a God who guides us according to his plans and has promised to never leave us. Therefore, as Paul wrote to the believers in Rome nearly two-thousand years ago, may the God of hope fill you with all joy and peace in believing, so that you will abound in hope by the power of the Holy Spirit. (Rom 15:13).

The New Creation

In my previous youth group, we once had a time discussing our favourite throw-away verses. Verses which appear to be insignificant and so are typically ignored, but which, upon closer examination, are incredibly profound. The complex imagery found in Revelation results in many such verses that likely won't resonate with us, but that would have immediately caught the attention of an ancient reader. Below are three which summarise the significance of the new creation:

there is no longer any sea (Rev 21:1)

In the ancient world the sea symbolised chaos and disorder, states also associated with sickness and suffering. The initial form of the earth is sea (Gen 1:2) before God brings forth land and vegetation. The Bible presents God as a force of order and therefore a creation with no sea means that all ungodliness has been wiped away. All sickness, pain and death are removed and all that's left is creation as God intended.

its length and width and height are equal (Rev 21:16)

This verse describes the new city of Jerusalem and its significance found by looking back to the description of Solomon's temple. The Holy of Holies was where God dwelt within this building and was likewise shaped in the form of a cube (1 Kings 6:20). In the new creation there is no temple building. Instead, the whole earth is God's temple and the new Jerusalem his dwelling place. We're no longer separated from God, but dwell alongside him as was the case in the Garden of Eden.

they will see his face (Rev 22:4)

A final verse to consider refers to the time of Moses. When asked what he desired from God, Moses replied that he wished to see his face. However, that was the one thing he could never receive as no one can look upon the face of God and live (Ex 33:20). And yet in the future, with creation fully redeemed, we're promised that we'll be able to do what even Moses could not. The separation that was caused by sin, which the system of sacrifice operated within and which was overcome by the death and resurrection of Jesus will finally be no more. We shall reign alongside our Lord and king for all eternity. This is how the story of the Bible ends, the greatest story ever told.

Appendix: Literary Styles of the Bible

As has been mentioned on several occasions previously, the Bible is a collection of 66 books comprised of different literary styles, written to various audiences, and covering around two thousand years of history. All these facts make understanding the Bible challenging. With regards to the latter two points, we need to recognize that the original audience being addressed are different not just from our own culture, but perhaps also different from the people another part of the Bible was written to. Some of these differences are obvious such as the Galatians clearly being a different group of people to the Ephesians. Others are less so, such as the books of Hosea and Micah addressing different groups of Israelites (Israel and Judah) after the separation of the kingdom. We should also be alert to cultural developments in Israel. For example, the religious structures of Israel during the gospels are far removed from what we see in Israel during the Old Testament.

The work of historians and theologians can greatly help us in identifying the historical and cultural contexts behind a passage and therefore better understand the text before us. However, although such considerations can be incredibly beneficial, it's worth remembering that one could spend a lifetime studying a given book of the Bible without ever encountering all there is to discover. Therefore, something that's in my view far more achievable for us when reading the Bible is to consider the first point mentioned above – the literary style of the passage being read. If we were to read a poem and a diary entry from a soldier that both described the Battle of the Somme, we would hopefully recognise that we should interpret them in different ways. Poems tend to be filled with symbolism and have a very deliberate construction that seeks to emphasise particular feelings or events to evoke an emotional response. On the other hand, a diary entry provides a chronological account that is likely more akin to a photographic depiction of what took place, but that may also be a somewhat biased interpretation, informed more by emotion than objectivity. The point here isn't to dwell upon how reliable each type of literature is, but simply highlight the differences in how we should approach them.

The same is true of the various literary styles in the Bible. Prophetic texts should be interpreted differently from psalms that should likewise be interpreted differently from narrative. On the following pages are brief descriptions of the major literary styles found within the Bible and several tips to consider when you encounter them. Hopefully through them, your times reading the Bible will become ever more fruitful.

Narrative / Historical

Narrative literature is probably the simplest form for us to understand, though that doesn't mean that there are no challenges. Narrative is an account of events, specifically God's interactions with Israel and her people and the decades surrounding the ministry of Jesus. It makes little attempt to explain finer points of theology or justify the actions recorded, with those tasks instead left to the reader. Most books in the Bible contain narrative elements, however the sections where the genre is predominantly found are the first seventeen books of the Old Testament and the first five of the New Testament.

All Events are Recorded for a Reason

The biblical narrative spans over two-thousand years of history and therefore the authors are selective with what they include. For example, the book of Judges covers hundreds of years of history in around 20 chapters. Similarly, from the middle of 1 Kings until the end of 2 Kings, time progresses by around four hundred years. At the opposite end of the spectrum, the roughly sixty chapters between Exodus 15 and Numbers 14 detail just a year or so. The primary purpose of these books isn't recording every piece of Israel's history. Instead, it's on recording specific interactions between Israel and God in order to demonstrate the person of God and the spiritual history of Israel to a future reader.

These books are theology first and foremost; history is the secondary role. In the case of Judges, stories are chosen not to preserve a record of conflicts but to highlight the idolatry of the people, the ramifications of this idolatry and God's faithfulness in spite of it. Additionally, in 1 and 2 Kings, the majority of the rulers of Israel and Judah have their reign summarised in just a few sentences. Those whose reigns are described in more detail tend to be those who played a significant role in the spiritual history of God's people such as Ahab, Hezekiah and Josiah.

This remains true as we move into the New Testament. Despite our cultural emphasis on Christmas and the nativity, two of the gospels don't record the birth of Jesus and passages about his childhood consist of just one account in Luke. The accounts of Jesus are focused on his ministry, death and resurrection – the key theological components of the biblical narrative. Whenever we read narrative, we should consider why these specific events have been recorded. What do they reveal about God? What do they reveal about the human condition? How does the author want us to respond to their words?

Description Isn't the Same as Affirmation

The individuals described in the Bible aren't heroes who we should perfectly imitate. For example, Jacob was a man who married twice and had children through four women. One could look at this account and conclude that God is encouraging us to engage in a polygamous lifestyle. However, Jacob's lifestyle is never commended and runs contrary to the rest of scripture that teaches the principle of monogamous marriage between man and wife. His family situation and favouritism of Joseph and Benjamin who had been born to him through Rachel were far from ideal and caused a great deal of heartache to everyone involved

The Bible repeatedly teaches that people are inherently sinful, and so although the people within may have traits that we should seek to emulate, they certainly all have weaknesses we should avoid. Samson was a womaniser, David murdered to cover up his adultery and Jonah wished death upon himself rather than see the Ninevites respond to God's call. For me, one of the most encouraging things to observe when reading the Bible is how God makes use of people who are just as flawed as we are to accomplish his purposes.

The Lesson is Left for us to Determine

Narrative concerns itself with what has happened but tends not to dwell on how the events described should inform our lives. For example, when the Israelites are being disciplined by God in the wilderness, there are no accompanying explanations of the lessons that future generations should take. (Paul does so much later in 1 Corinthians 10:1-13 but the source text is silent.) Sometimes the lesson is obvious; often it is less so and frequently there are multiple truths that could be pulled out. Ask two people to preach on the same passage and it is unlikely they will say the same thing.

When seeking to identify any principles the author wished to convey, it can be helpful to consider the surrounding passages, or any themes of the book which seem to be frequently appearing. 1 Samuel 13-15 records three events from the reign of Saul which together serve to demonstrate his failure as a spiritual leader for the people. On a larger scale, the book of Joshua is focused upon the faithfulness of God and the expectation that the Israelites remain faithful to him. The events which the author chooses to describe tend to be reinforcing these principles.

It is Ancient History

The history described in these books is recorded differently to how we might expect, particularly having grown accustomed to a historical method that places a premium on accuracy and attention to detail. Numbers are sometimes rounded, and quotations aren't necessarily exact. Also, due to a lack of knowledge that modern readers now possess, events are recorded in ways that an ancient reader would have understood. For example, the Old Testament frequently uses language that was in line with their cosmological view of the heavens and earth (God above, bodies of water above and below the land, the sun moving relative to the earth, etc).

There are also literary devices that ancient writers used that we should be aware of. For example, it was common when recounting battles to use hyperbolic language that overstated a victory, something particularly relevant to the Old Testament's accounts of warfare. Joshua 10:36-40 describes the utter destruction of Canaanites in six regions, but at the start of Judges (1:1) they're still present in at least five! Clearly the first verse was hyperbolic.

Another feature to be aware of is the attributing of everything to the gods. Ultimately there's a lot of truth in this idea but it can still cloud interpretation. An ancient would see any negative outcome as a punishment sent from God. However, it may be that certain sufferings the Israelites experienced weren't a form of discipline but rather the consequences of ignoring God's instructions. An analogy would be ignoring the speed limit when driving. By speeding you're of course more likely to receive a criminal punishment but you are also more likely to injure yourself in an accident.

But it's Still History

Although selective, and occasionally written in ways we aren't familiar with, the Biblical narrative is still describing historical events. David was a real person who fought a real person in Goliath, succeeded a real person in Saul as king of Israel, was father to a real son in Solomon and really did write at least 75 Psalms. It's easy to dismiss certain stories as impossible because of what is described, but we worship a supernatural God. Therefore, how can we possibly claim that Jesus could not walk on water, or that God couldn't cause the sun to stop in the sky without the world falling apart (on the last point I find it interesting that so many ancient cultures possess a legend of an extraordinarily long day / night).

Law

Law is a literary style comprised mostly of lists of instructions and rules. For this reason, it can be quite repetitive and, perhaps, even tiresome to read. However, contained within are amazing revelations about the person of God and what he desires of those who worship him. It's striking that despite having a reputation as one of the hardest (and most boring) books found in the Bible, Leviticus was the first book that an Israelite child would have learned to recite.

For the Israelites, the purposes of legal literature were:

1. Providing a legal framework for the nation of Israel.
2. Detailing what their worship should look like.
3. Outlining the covenantal requirements of Israel.
4. Exposing their sin and shortcomings before God.
5. Further revealing the nature of God.

This literary style is primarily found in the second half of Exodus, Leviticus, parts of Numbers and Deuteronomy (a name that literally means Second Law).

Focus on God

All scripture is God's revelation to us and therefore it can be helpful to focus our attention less on how the law would have functioned and more on what these laws reveal about God and his expectations for us. A good example of this is the idea of an eye for an eye (Ex 21:23-25). This isn't teaching that if someone strikes us we are obligated to do the same, or that we have a God given right to do so. Instead, the law is primarily demonstrating God's desire for proportionate punishment in a dispute rather than vengeful attitudes and an escalation in revenge (you stole my sheep so I killed your ox and then you killed my son so now I'm going to kill your whole family).

This can also help inform our conduct in areas not mentioned by scripture. For example, both Old Testament legal literature and New Testament teaching has much to say about sexual conduct, and God's expectations of us in this area, that is often far removed from modern attitudes. Jesus tells people not just to avoid adultery, but to avoid even lustful thoughts! This aspect of our lives is clearly important to God and therefore we can use these principles to conclude that actions such as the viewing of pornography are clearly contrary to God's will even though they aren't specifically mentioned.

There are Different Types of Laws

It can be helpful to think of the laws given to Israel as consisting of three types. Ceremonial laws demonstrate what Israelite worship should look like and are therefore interested in sacrifice, the priests, tabernacle rituals and personal purity. With the death and resurrection of Jesus we are no longer obliged to keep these laws. Civil laws are rules that lay out how Israelite society should function. When the festivals should take place, how certain disputes should be resolved, how people should be treated in given situations. Again, as we do not live in ancient Israel, we are not expected to adhere to these specific laws. Finally, there are moral laws which outline how people should behave. Falling in this category would be the second half of the ten commandments, the laws governing sexual conduct and similar prohibitions. These moral principles are the same today as they were to the Israelites three and a half thousand years ago.

Classifying laws according to this model can be a helpful way to understand how we should respond to the different laws given to Israel. However, because the original text doesn't group laws in this way, that task is left for us. Something that is central to this process is considering the regulations in light of the rest of scripture - specifically the New Testament. The laws of the Old Testament are given to Israel in order for them to maintain their access to the blessings of the covenant. However, as Christians we've entered into a different covenant established through the blood of Christ. Therefore, when Jesus or one of the apostles are commanding their audience to behave in a certain way, they are appealing to a morality that transcends the original covenant made with Israel. Commands to abstain from sexual immorality (1 Cor 6:9), envy (Gal 5:21), anger (Matt 5:22), *aren't given because of a law given to Israel*, but because God desires these actions of all people. We can therefore use the moral teachings of the New Testament to identify moral teaching from the Old Covenant that we should seek to follow today.

A final point is that even if we're not required to exactly keep the ceremonial and civil laws, that doesn't mean they are absent of value to us. In fact, many helpful principles can be drawn from them and applied to our own lives. The ceremonial laws can serve as a reminder that we worship a holy God, and that our sin is something we should seek to correct. Similarly, the civil laws demonstrate a form of social justice where people are treated with respect and fairness - both values that we should be trying to uphold in our interactions with others.

Certain Laws are Case Studies

Exodus 21:33-34 states that if someone digs a pit and, due to not covering it, a neighbour's ox or donkey falls in, the owner of the pit must pay reparations to the owner of the ox. What about if it was a neighbour's sheep though? Or goat? Despite not being stated here, any judge presiding over such a case would be able to use this law as an example of what should happen. The heart of this law is making sure that people are held responsible for negligent actions (leaving the pit uncovered) that impact an innocent third party. The animal mentioned, and arguably the pit too, are merely examples from which principles of justice can be drawn. Therefore, the pit owner would still have been required to pay the owner of the animal.

The Laws were Given to a Different Culture

Although many laws are straight forward to understand (don't murder people, don't steal, etc), some can sound quite peculiar. For example, not wearing clothes made of two materials (Lev 19:19) or the prohibitions surrounding haircuts and tattoos (Lev 19:27). As a twenty-first century Christian, these sorts of laws can be confusing and are therefore often the target of mockery from unbelievers.

Something that can help in understanding what God was saying through these laws is focusing upon how the Israelites would have interpreted them. By studying the surrounding cultures, we can conclude that it's likely they were intended to prevent the Israelites imitating the spiritual customs of their neighbours. The ban on mixed fabric clothing targeted fertility cult practices performed by Canaanites as a form of sympathetic magic. The haircuts were sometimes crafted to worship other gods, but the law is also likely setting guidelines for mourning (as with v28) as mutilating oneself and having certain haircuts was a way of grieving in the ancient world.

Typically, a small amount of research, or investing in a good study Bible or commentary, can shed light onto the meaning behind a law we don't fully understand. However, irrespective of whether we can determine for certain what issues the law was addressing, we can be confident that the laws would have made perfect sense to the Israelites.

Poetic

Poetry is, besides narrative, the most common literary style found in the Bible and is the genre most similar to its modern equivalent. Symbolism and imagery are used abundantly to convey truths in a more memorable and concise way than would be achieved in a book of theology and, perhaps, with the intention of evoking an emotional response. The key feature of ancient poetry, and the thing that most distinguishes it from contemporary poetry is parallelism, something described in more detail below.

Psalms, Lamentations and Song of Songs are books of poetry. However, this literary style is also prevalent in the prophets, wisdom literature, and occasionally appears too alongside historical passages. Wherever poetry appears the tips below can be helpful in interpreting the text.

Parallelism is Everywhere

Parallelism is the defining feature of ancient poetry and describes a literary technique of writing sequential lines that are directly related to one another. Several forms of parallelism which appear in the Bible are listed below.

Synonymous

Lines that contain the same (or a similar) thought in different words.

For I will not trust in my bow,
Nor will my sword save me (Psalm 44:6)

Antithetic

Lines that contain contrasting thoughts.

For the Lord knows the way of the righteous,
But the way of the wicked will perish (Psalm 1:6)

Synthetic

Lines that build upon one another.

It is better to listen to the rebuke of a wise man
Than for one to listen to the song of fools. (Ecclesiastes 7:5).

Emblematic

Lines where a simile or metaphor is expressed more literally in the other. Although similar to synonymous parallelism, the lines here don't just contain the same concept but are reliant upon one another. Therefore, the concept only becomes clear having read both.

Like apples of gold in settings of silver
Is a word spoken in right circumstances. (Proverbs 25:11).

Climactic

A series of lines building upon one another to a crescendo of thought.

Ascribe to the Lord, O sons of the mighty,
Ascribe to the Lord glory and strength.
Ascribe to the Lord the glory due to His name;
Worship the Lord in holy array. (Psalm 29: 1-2).

By identifying this feature and how small sections of a passage are related, we can better understand the point the author intended to make. For example, with synonymous parallelism the lines are generally intended to provide a more fleshed out image than could be achieved by only looking at either half independently. Similarly, with synthetic parallelism, we need to consider both parts before attempting to understand what the author was trying to convey.

Many are the afflictions of the righteous
but the Lord delivers him out of them all (Psalm 34:19).

The Bible calls us to be righteous and so the first part of this verse can seem horrifying! Should we conclude from this verse that our obedience will simply lead to many afflictions? The answer is found in the second line. Ultimately, all people suffer afflictions, but what distinguishes the righteous from others is that they have the assurance of a God beside them through it all.

There is Purpose Behind the Imagery

As previously mentioned, poetry in the Bible is filled with imagery and symbolism that has been deliberately chosen to convey information to the reader. Therefore, when reading poetry, it's helpful to spend time reflecting on the reasons behind the different imagery being used (both the lessons and emotional response that the author wished to convey) as opposed to reading through it quickly as we may do with narrative.

Psalm 23 begins with the well-known declaration that the Lord is my shepherd. What does it mean that God is our shepherd? Shepherds have a range of different roles including protecting their flock, guiding them according to their interests and providing for them – all characteristics that God too demonstrates towards us. God being our shepherd also carries with it the implication of us being part of a flock. Here we find a whole different set of teachings. A flock of sheep are utterly dependent upon their shepherd, incapable of making it home without his help. If we're a flock of sheep, then perhaps those traits are also found in us.

Sometimes Linked to Specific Events

Occasionally, a passage is written to address a specific situation which, when known, can assist us in understanding what the author was hoping to convey. For example, the poems in Lamentations are all written after the destruction of Jerusalem by the Babylonians. The author wrestles with the fact that this is God's judgement upon the nation and that it would never have happened had the people remained faithful to the covenant. And yet, amidst this pain, we have verses in the middle of the third chapter (v21-25) that remind the reader of God's great love and mercy towards his people. These verses become all the more powerful when read against the historical backdrop of the book.

In a similar way Psalm 51 was written by David after being confronted by the prophet Nathan about his sin with Bathsheba (2 Samuel 11-12). When we read this psalm in light of this historical context (and his greater journey that has led him to become king of Israel), we see a man who fully understands the severity of his actions and how he has failed God. Someone who wants God to transform his heart and lead him to become a better representative of the one who had placed him upon the throne.

Deliberately Structured

Something that distinguishes poetry from most other literary styles is a very deliberate focus upon structure. Some structural elements, such as rhythm and rhyme, are extremely hard to identify, however there are two key structures that are worth looking out for.

Certain passages are acrostics meaning that sequential lines (or sets of lines) start with sequential letters of the Hebrew alphabet, beginning with the first and ending with the last. Along with making the passage easier to recite, a key reason behind this structure is likely to do with signifying completeness. Psalm 145 details how worthy of praise God is. Although certain actions and aspects of his character are highlighted, the acrostic structure acts to further demonstrate how God is worthy of praise in all things.

Another important literary technique from a perspective of study is chiastic structure. This describes a train of thought where the first and last thoughts are related, the second and penultimate are related and so on until you reach the centre. The relationship may be complimentary, contrasting or building upon one another, however there will always be a thematic relationship between sections with key words or phrases also often repeated.

Psalm 47 is an example of such a psalm. It begins and ends with a gathering of peoples (verse 1 and 9), then has a statement about God's lordship over the earth (verses 2-4 and 8) whilst the three central verses describe how we should praise God.

Most literature we encounter today has a linear progression of thought. One idea introducing another before reaching the conclusion that we should remember. However, chiastic literature is typically emphasising the thought at the centre. For example, Leviticus has a chiastic structure with the central section describing the day of atonement – the most important event in Israel's religious calendar.

Chiastic structures are found throughout the Bible and, as the example above demonstrates, can be far larger and more complex than just a few verses. John's gospel contains various chiasms, as do Paul's letters. Ruth too is chiastic and also includes various smaller chiasms within the larger chiasm.

Wisdom

Wisdom literature was a common style of writing in the ancient world that sought to make sense of the world. However, what distinguishes the wisdom found in the Bible from elsewhere is that the Bible sees God as the source of all wisdom (Prov 9:10).

It's a varied genre but most wisdom found in the Bible can be placed into one of two major groups:

1. Passages that try to make sense of life by considering the big questions of life and / or major theological issues such as the things that are important in life (Ecclesiastes) and why the righteous suffer (Job).

2. Passages that seek to provide advice for how to best get through life (Proverbs, Song of Songs).

Along with the books listed above, certain psalms (or parts of a psalm) can also be classified as wisdom literature.

Wisdom and Foolishness

The Bible sees two paths that a person can walk: the way of the wise (or righteous) and the way of the fool (or wicked). To ignore the teachings that are found in wisdom literature means that one is walking the foolish path whilst adhering to them means they are living wisely. It's important to emphasise that wisdom is very different to intelligence and therefore the fool isn't necessarily academically inferior to someone classed as wise. Wisdom literature is instead concerned with informing our behaviour and teaching a particular way of life.

Some Wisdom Literature Needs to be Considered as a Whole

The book of Proverbs is filled with short statements of wisdom which typically make sense by themselves. However, Ecclesiastes and Job are very different. Both work through some of life's big questions and, in doing so, various thoughts are presented which are later explained to be false. Some of these misconceptions are very relatable to either our own beliefs or the beliefs of others in the church and therefore it's helpful that the Bible addresses them. However, in order to fully understand what the author is seeking to convey, we need to read the whole book before drawing conclusions.

Wisdom Literatures Teaches Principles – It Doesn't Make Guarantees

Wisdom literature doesn't provide guarantees for life. Instead, it teaches principles that should shape our behaviour and which, when followed, are likely to benefit us. For example:

Do not love sleep, or you will become poor;
Open your eyes, and you will be satisfied with food. (Proverbs 20:13).

Our own observations of the world tell us that there are exceptions to this principle. However, in general, it's true that people will accomplish far more through hard work than a lazy, apathetic attitude.

Another example is found in this seemingly contradictory passage:

Do not answer a fool according to his folly,
Or you will also be like him.
Answer a fool as his folly deserves,
That he not be wise in his own eyes. (Proverbs 26:4-5).

Both sayings are grounded in truth. We should definitely seek to correct the foolish beliefs of others, but there will also be times where their lack of desire to listen to correction mean that it's not worth wasting time replying. As the reader we're expected to understand when these principles should apply and how best to act in a given situation.

The Retribution Principle

Another idea found in these books is the retribution principle. In summary, this is the idea that the righteous prosper and the wicked suffer in proportion to their actions. If God is just, we would expect this to be broadly true and therefore a major theological question within the Israelite culture, and sometimes ours today, is why there are times when the righteous suffer and the wicked prosper? This is the key question Job and his friends were wrestling with.

The Old Testament was written before Jesus or the final judgement had been revealed, meaning that the Israelite's view of justice was more limited to earthly gains and losses. Some of the more challenging Psalms for us to understand have David calling on God to punish his oppressors. However, when seen through the lens of the retribution principle, it becomes clearer as to why David is asking this of God. He is asking God to demonstrate his justice.

Prophecy

When people hear the word prophecy what often comes to mind are predictions for the future. However, although such descriptions are an element of prophecy, the ultimate purpose of a prophet is to speak God's message to his people. Therefore, although some prophetic books contain predictive elements, they all record instances where God speaks to a specific group of people about a specific situation through a God appointed prophet.

Typically passages of prophecy can be put into one of four groups:

1. Exposing the covenant failures of the people.
2. The judgement that they should expect if they do not repent (change their ways).
3. Instruction concerning how the people should conduct themselves.
4. The hope and future blessings that God has in store for his faithful followers.

The final 17 books of the Old Testament, excluding Lamentations and Jonah, are prophetic. Lamentations is placed with the prophets because it is typically thought to have been authored by Jeremiah. Jonah too is included amongst the prophetic books because its author was a prophet.

Know the Context

Books of prophecy record God's words to his people at various situations. Ezekiel speaks to those effected by the Babylonian conquest. Hosea to the people of Israel before their conquest by Assyria. Haggai to those who have returned from exile. Because each prophecy is addressed to people at a specific time or period, it's important to know what was taking place when the prophecy was given. Through this information it becomes easier for us to understand the points God was making to the original recipients, and the lessons that we can draw from the text and apply to our lives today. (A simple list outlining the context of each prophetic book can be found on pages 81-85).

An additional challenge is that some prophetic books cover a large span of time, particularly the three major prophets: Isaiah, Jeremiah and Ezekiel. Diligent study of the scriptures and the history of Israel that they record will of course help with identifying the events associated with a specific prophetic word. However, if you lack such knowledge then the cross references included by a study Bible or a commentary of the book will be of great benefit to you.

It was Written to an Audience in their Language

When reading the Bible, it's important to remember that it's not written to us but to a people who lived thousands of years ago and possessed their own culture and language. Although modern translations do a great job of conveying the original message, we can still face challenges when encountering concepts that are alien to us.

An example of this is the day of the Lord, a phrase repeated in many of the prophets and something that refers to multiple events individually or all at once. It can refer to God intervening in a present problem that the people are experiencing or be speaking of events in the far future such as the arrival of Israel's messiah or the end of time when God restores all things.

Focus on God, Not the Future

Although there are many cases of the prophets predicting the future, the primary purpose of the text isn't foretelling what will occur but speaking God's word to the people about their current situation. Isaiah speaks to the nation under Hezekiah as the Assyrian army bears down upon them, Jeremiah to those who have just been cast out of Jerusalem and Haggai to those who are struggling to rebuild the temple upon their return from Babylon. Although each book contains comments about the future, the bulk of the text is addressing the current predicament that the people find themselves in.

Trying to tie prophecies of the future to specific events is rarely helpful and not always possible. It's easy to perceive prophecies as talking about us or modern Israel, however most were fulfilled before or during the ministry of Jesus. Some predictions are quite generic, and fulfilment is also not always linked to one event. The abomination that causes desolation of Daniel 12:11 can be linked to both the defilement of the temple by Antiochus (p95) and the Roman destruction of the temple in 70AD.

Instead of looking into the future, our focus should be seeing what the prophecy is revealing to us about God. Because the prophets are recording the words of God, we are provided with a window into his heart in the same way that Jesus does in the gospels. Through these books we encounter a God who cares about justice, who abhors sin and evil, who loves his people and is faithful to his promises.

Apocalyptic

Apocalyptic literature is something that is completely alien to us as modern readers and so is probably the most challenging genre for us to understand. Although apocalypse tends to be used today in relation to the end of the world, the term ultimately refers to an unveiling of things that are hidden. Typically, this is carried out by means of a heavenly visitor revealing things of the spiritual realm which are then recorded by a prophet. As the message is coming from God, the genre is very similar to prophecy but tends to be primarily focused on things of the future, relying far more on symbolism and imagery.

Daniel, Ezekiel and Zechariah each contain significant amounts of apocalyptic text, whilst Revelation is almost entirely apocalyptic. Jesus's words on signs that will accompany the end of the age are also apocalyptic, although, being God, he doesn't need a third party to provide revelation in the same way that humans do.

Appreciate the Prevalence of Symbolism

Over the history of the church many believers have tried link the book of Revelation to various global events and predict what will occur in the future. The biggest challenge for us as readers is understanding that apocalyptic visions are full of imagery and symbolism that can be hard to identify and harder still to understand. Therefore, they shouldn't be thought of as eyewitness accounts. Symbolism is a controversial word at times, mainly due to the way it can be abused to explain away difficult parts of the Bible such as the resurrection. Clearly to do this is to go too far, but in order to read apocalyptic text we need to understand that it's not historical literature and that symbolism is everywhere.

A lot of symbolism can be understood by identifying connections with other passages of scripture. An example is found in the description of the New Jerusalem (Revelation 21). The city is described as 12,000 stadia (around 1400 miles) wide, long and high. The wall was 144 cubits (65m) thick. Lots of numbers in apocalyptic texts are symbolic and based around key biblical numbers such as 12 (tribes of Israel, disciples of Jesus), and mathematical operations including squaring a number and multiplying it by 1000, both of which are found in this chapter. Similar cubic dimensions are also found in the Old Testament when describing the Holy of Holies where God dwelt among his people as he will in the new Jerusalem.

Apocalyptic Literature is Still Revealing God

Although it may be exciting to understand exactly what these various passages are describing, the reason that they're in the Bible is primarily to reveal God to us. Revelation is written to an increasingly persecuted church who have seen its leaders martyred for their faith. Therefore, at the heart of the book is a reminder to the church that, above all they're experiencing, God reigns. He is in control and is assured the final victory. Upon his return this earth will be transformed so that death and pain are finally silenced. This message of hope is far more important to understand than questioning what the mark of the beast is or who the Anti-Christ may or may not be.

Approach with Humility

Because these texts are so difficult to study, we need to approach them with humility. God has blessed the church with people who have spent a lifetime studying these parts of the Bible and it would therefore be foolish of us to ignore what they have to say. We should seek guidance from scholars who understand this literary style and be open to the beliefs of others. We should also recognise that some questions are unanswerable this side of heaven. Arguments have raged on certain issues for centuries, but ultimately, the truth with only be revealed when Jesus returns. Therefore, most disputes over interpretation of these texts aren't worth jeopardising fellowship and unity over.

Gospel

Gospels are a subsection of the larger historical genre and record the ministry of Jesus and the good news (gospel) that he proclaims. The first four books of the New Testament are gospels. Although they all focus on Jesus, their authors each have a slightly different point of emphasis leading to the inclusion (or emission) of certain events.

The first three gospels are known as the Synoptic Gospels due to the similarities between them in providing a fast-paced overview of Jesus's ministry. The first, Matthew, presents Jesus as Israel's Messiah and, through the language and details used, appears to be writing to a largely Jewish audience. The accounts of Jesus are grouped thematically rather than chronologically. The apostle Matthew is the most likely author.

The second Synoptic Gospel is Mark which focuses on Jesus being our Great High Priest and the Messiah in the model of the suffering servant proclaimed by Isaiah. The Messiah was expected to lead Israel into battle, but Mark emphasises instead, through the prophecies of Isaiah, that the Messiah was more concerned with the sins of the world. It is the shortest of the gospels moving quickly from one story to the next. The book is credited to Mark (perhaps John Mark who appears in the book of Acts) and is thought to be largely based upon the eyewitness testimonies of Peter.

Luke is the final Synoptic Gospel and is focused on Jesus being the Saviour of the world. Therefore, it includes more of Jesus's interactions with foreigners (Gentiles) and women - both marginalised groups. Like Mark, events are ordered chronologically. Luke identifies himself as the author and is the same Luke who wrote Acts and accompanied Paul during some of his ministry.

John is the final gospel contained in the Bible and is very different from the Synoptics. For example, there are no parables and many of the events recorded aren't found in the other gospels. This is likely due to it being the final gospel written and therefore having no need to repeat what people already knew. Another difference is the inclusion of more lengthy discourses between Jesus and various parties. It's focused on Jesus being the Son of God and most explicitly connects Jesus with the temple system. He's described as dwelling among us, but the word dwell is more accurately translated as tabernacled, thus highlighting John's key point that Jesus is God revealed in flesh. It is widely thought to have been written by the apostle John.

Each Gospel has a Purpose

As mentioned above, each gospel has a slightly different focus that can help us to understand the purpose behind accounts and why certain passages appear in only some, or one, of the gospels. For example, John tells us exactly why he wrote his gospel - to convince us that Jesus was the Son of God (John 20:31). Therefore, everything in his gospel should be read with that intention in mind.

On the other hand, Luke, whose focus is on Jesus being the Saviour of the World, includes more accounts of Jesus's interactions with women and groups looked down upon by the Jews, Simeon's words over Jesus (2:28-32), and the parable of the Good Samaritan (10:30-37). There are many reasons these passages are included but at least one is to reinforce Luke's big themes.

The Gospels Assume Certain Knowledge

The Gospels are addressed to a group who lived within a generation of Jesus's ministry. Therefore, they continually assume the reader knows what is happening in the present as well as the events of their nation's history. Consequently, in order that we don't overlook details of his ministry, we need to recognise that Jesus taught in a world radically different to that of the Old Testament (p95-96). The Pharisees come across as the villains of the gospels, with Jesus regularly challenging them over their behaviours. However, they were also well supported by the public. This point helps to explains why Jesus was so keen to address their errors, but it also explains why the people were reluctant to accept what Jesus was saying to them. When you're taught something your whole life by people you trust and someone comes along with a radically different perspective, who are you likely to agree with?

Turning attention to the past, having knowledge of the Old Testament also helps us to understand the ministry of Jesus. He is the fulfilment of numerous prophecies, signals the end of the sacrificial system and identifies himself as the Messiah whom Israel have waited generations for. Because the writers assume their audience are familiar with the Old Testament, many questions that we have aren't directly addressed. Why were Samaritans hated so much? Why was the temple such a big deal and why was it so abhorrent for the priests to be selling birds? Why did people expect Jesus to overthrow the Romans? Why was Jesus forgiving people so scandalous? All of these are best answered through knowing the history and scripture that preceded Jesus.

The Narrative is Deliberately Structured

As with all biblical history, the gospels are selective in what they include (John 21:25) meaning there is always a reason behind what is recorded. The overall theme of the gospel plays a big role in these choices, but another technique used by the authors is the grouping of accounts that convey a similar message. This is found in each of the gospels, but it's perhaps most obvious in Matthew where the content is frequently arranged thematically, not chronologically. For example, chapters 8 through 12 are Matthew's revelation to his readers of the Lordship of Jesus. He is Lord over sickness (8:1-4), Lord of the Gentiles (8:5-13), Lord over creation (8:23-27), Lord over the spiritual realm (8:28-34), Lord of forgiveness (9:1-8), Lord of Sinners (9:9-13), Lord of a new and better promise (9:14-17), Lord over death (9:18-26), Lord of the harvest (9:35-38), and Lord of the Sabbath, in other words, our Lord God (12:1-14). In isolation they each reveal an aspect of Jesus. However, taken together, we can see the complete Lordship of Jesus over all things that Matthew is trying to convey (Col 1:15-20, Heb 1:1-3).

Surrounding verses and events can also be illuminating. Luke 15 records the parables of the lost sheep, lost coin and lost (prodigal) son placed consecutively. All three of these parables are concerned with God's love for the returning sinner but use different imagery to reveal multiple points to the listener. If we are wanting to study this topic in detail, then we should consider these parables collectively, examining common themes present in each and how the specific details of each parable fit together. Limiting study to just the parable of the lost sheep could lead us to think that God comes and finds us without us having to do anything. Focusing on just the prodigal son could lead to the opposite conclusion, that we must come to our senses ourselves and head back to God. Taken together though, along with the rest of scripture, we see that there is truth in both parables. God does come searching after us wherever we are and the Holy Spirit works to bring us to place of repentance, yet we still have a responsibility to answer his call.

Parables were Spoken to an Ancient Audience

Parables are a means of communicating spiritual matters through story and imagery. They were one of the primary methods of teaching employed by Jesus and so, although absent from John's gospel, a large amount of what Jesus says is delivered in this form. Alongside the more general advice to understanding the gospels discussed above, there are several additional points that we should consider when reading parables.

Firstly, most parables are spoken as a response to a question or particular situation. By identifying why a parable was spoken, it becomes easier to identify the key issues Jesus was looking to address, and the major points that he wanted to convey to his listeners. It's also worth noting that because they are emphasising certain points, they don't always convey a perfect picture of God or an action we should perform. In the parable of the persistent widow the key point is that we should be persistent in prayer not that God is a reluctant giver who we have to wear down as the widow does the judge.

Secondly, certain imagery is used in multiple parables to represent the same individuals or groups. Israel is often represented by a vineyard, God by a king or judge. Believers are associated with sheep whilst the wicked are represented by goats. Many of these images are found in the Old Testament as well which again demonstrates how parables are told in ways that Jesus's audience would have understood.

On this point, there are many small details that would have resonated with them that we may miss. In the parable of the wedding banquet, the excuses people give for not turning up are ridiculous and therefore Jesus is charging people with ignoring the gospel message for no good reason. He's not speaking harshly of those who have not heard of him or are wrestling with doubts. In the parable of the prodigal son the father rushes out to meet him. For a wealthy father to do this would have been incredibly shameful and so this description demonstrates the abundant love that God has for us. One that meant he was prepared to die in the most shameful way the Romans had devised, in order to rescue the world from sin and death. There is of course a danger that we dig too deep looking for details and see things that were never intended. For example, the famine is likely a device which progresses the narrative being told rather than a specific detail we should obsess over. However, such mistakes don't negate the fact that there are many details found in the parables that we are often oblivious to.

Epistle

Epistles are letters written to Christians in the early church and are in a way the New Testament's version of prophecy, the difference being that the words recorded are not (apart from Revelation 1-3) directly from the mouth of God. The final 22 books of the New Testament are epistles, with the majority written by either Paul or another major figure of the early church. They were written to encourage, challenge and teach churches or people whilst the author was ministering elsewhere. The letters addressed pastoral and theological issues which the people were wrestling with and, as they were almost all written within 20 – 40 years of Jesus, provide a remarkable window into the beliefs, disputes and pressures experienced by the first sets of believers.

They Are Designed to be Studied as a Whole

More than any of the literary styles previously discussed, epistles should be read and evaluated as a whole. For our convenience they've been divided into chapters and sections, but the original readers would have read them as one large piece of text. Arguments tend to build upon one another and therefore it's very challenging to evaluate verses, or even chapters, in isolation from the rest of the text. For example, the first eight chapters of Romans are Paul's presentation of the gospel, from humanity's disposition to sin, our inability to save ourselves, the saving work of God and, finally, the consequences for our lives. Similarly, Hebrews builds upon itself as the priestly role of Christ is explored in increasing detail.

Another reason to read passages in larger sections is that certain divisions are particularly unhelpful. In Romans 1, Paul lists the sinful actions of the Gentiles before ending with a far more extensive list of immoral behaviour. The reason for this is found in the first verse of Romans 2. A Jewish reader would have been in complete agreement with Paul's condemnation of the idolatrous lifestyles of the Gentiles, but as Paul goes through his larger list, it would have been impossible for them to not be convicted by at least one of the words there. Who hasn't felt greed? Or been disobedient? Paul has laid his trap and then, as Romans 2 begins, he springs it. How can you judge others when you yourself do the same things? This is all part of his larger argument that there is no distinction between Jew and Gentile. We have all sinned and fall short of God's glory (Rom 3:23). Rather than building theologies around verses or short passages we need to consider the text as a whole.

Written to Specific People(s) in Specific Situations

These books are written to specific people(s) in specific situations and therefore, to understand what the author wished to communicate, we need to consider the background of each letter. What questions were being addressed? What was happening when the letter was written? By whom and where would this letter have been read? What cultural elements were specific to that location?

There are also images that would make sense to a first century recipient that are not necessarily obvious to us. Rev 3:15 talks of the Laodicean church being lukewarm and God wanting them to be hot or cold. On first glance this can seem an odd thing for God to say. He would rather they were cold towards him? However, this image is a reference to the Greek custom of serving wine hot or cold. Wine served lukewarm was an insult to your guest and worthy of being spat out (v16). The church is being charged with receiving Christ in this way and are therefore instructed to get their priorities straight, responding to him as a host would treat an honoured guest.

Old Testament Quotations

The New Testament authors frequently quote the Old Testament and, occasionally, other ancient texts such as the apocryphal Book of Enoch (Jude 1:14-15). Although the reason behind a quotation is often clear it's still good practice to look at the context it was originally written in and the surrounding text. Paul's use of the Old Testament in Romans 10:5-8 can be quite perplexing upon first encountering it. However, what he is referencing is the end of Deuteronomy where God explained to the Israelites that he had revealed to them everything they needed, and that therefore they could either follow him or perish. The same was true for Paul's audience. Everything had been revealed to them in Christ and thus the same decision lay before them.

Typically, seeing the context of an Old Testament quotation will shed light on why it was used. However, one thing to be aware of is that the writers of the New Testament had a far greater knowledge of their scriptures (the Old Testament) than we tend to. Therefore, whenever passages are quoted, there is an underlying assumption that their reader will be aware of how that specific text is connected to similar concepts and passages found elsewhere.